D0667150

Economics for the Curious

ECONOMICS FOR THE CURIOUS

Inside the Minds
of 12 Nobel Laureates

Edited by
ROBERT M. SOLOW AND
JANICE MURRAY

palgrave
macmillan

First published 2014 by
PALGRAVE MACMILLAN

Palgrave Macmillan in the UK is an imprint of Macmillan Publishers Limited,
registered in England, company number 785998, of Houndmills, Basingstoke,
Hampshire RG21 6XS.

Palgrave Macmillan in the US is a division of St Martin's Press LLC,
175 Fifth Avenue, New York, NY 10010.

Palgrave Macmillan is the global academic imprint of the above companies
and has companies and representatives throughout the world.

Palgrave® and Macmillan® are registered trademarks in the United States,
the United Kingdom, Europe and other countries.

ISBN 978–1–137–38358–7

This book is printed on paper suitable for recycling and made from fully
managed and sustained forest sources. Logging, pulping and manufacturing
processes are expected to conform to the environmental regulations of the
country of origin.

A catalogue record for this book is available from the British Library.

A catalog record for this book is available from the Library of Congress.

Typeset by MPS Limited, Chennai, India.

330
ECO

18.70

This book is dedicated to Professor Wolfgang Schürer,
who started it all

CONTENTS

Acknowledgments   ix

Introduction   1

1   Depressions are Different   7
     Paul R. Krugman

2   Rethinking Economics: A Classical
     Perspective   19
     Vernon L. Smith

3   Employment and Unemployment   33
     Peter A. Diamond

4   Unemployment During and After the Great
     Recession   43
     Dale T. Mortensen

5   Long-Term Trends and Structural Changes
     in the Global Economy   61
     A. Michael Spence

6   On Policy Consistency   77
     Finn E. Kydland

7   Natural Resources and Sustainability   97
     Robert M. Solow

8   Research Studies Approaching Cooperative
       Games with New Methods   109
       John F. Nash Jr.

9   Interdisciplinary Social Science:
       The Transaction Cost Economics Project   123
       Oliver E. Williamson

10   Financing Retirement   141
       William F. Sharpe

11   How Should We Elect Our Leaders?   159
       Eric S. Maskin

12   Standards for State-Building Interventions   171
       Roger B. Myerson

Appendix A: List of Nobel Laureates   189

Appendix B: The Lindau Meetings   193

ACKNOWLEDGMENTS

Any book's production, from genesis to completion, needs and benefits from the involvement of many people. We wish to recognize those who gave much-needed support: Nikolaus Turner and Wolfgang Huang at the Lindau Nobel Laureates Meetings; Andreas Böhm; copy-editor Elizabeth Stone; and David Bull at Palgrave. We are especially grateful to Peter Badge for the portraits of the Laureates, and to Chris Richmond for preparing the biographies.

John G. Froemming of Jones Day, in Washington, DC and New York, was so generous with his time in providing legal counsel. Peter Baker at Palgrave graciously and patiently shepherded us through the process.

Last but not least, without financial support from the Foundation Lindau Nobelprizewinners Meetings at Lake Constance, and the inspiration and devotion to education of Wolfgang Schürer, this book would never have reached fruition.

Introduction

One standard definition of economics describes the field as the study of the allocation of scarce resources to alternative uses. That's accurate: if Adam and Eve had never left the Garden of Eden, they would never have needed an economist. But this sounds too dry, too abstract, to make economics seem like an exciting or interesting thing to learn about. Alfred Marshall, a great English economist of the late 19th century, used plainer but more enticing language: he said, more or less, that economics was the study of mankind in the ordinary business of earning a living. Anyone with reasonable curiosity would be, or should be, interested in learning about that. The idea for this book, which came from Professor Wolfgang Schürer, was to provide students near the beginning of their academic lives with a sampling of the sorts of problem that a group of pretty good economists – winners of the Nobel Prize, in fact – found it interesting and useful *and possible* to think about productively. What he and we hope is that some of those who read this book will be tempted to study economics, either professionally or because they find it interesting and important as citizens, whatever their professions.

A look at the Table of Contents will show that the 'ordinary business of earning a living' seems to cover a very wide range of activities. Eric Maskin discusses alternative ways of counting votes in an election; and Roger Myerson considers political processes on a much larger scale. How did economics come to include such things? Here is one possible rationalization.

If we date economics from the time of Adam Smith (although of course Smith had predecessors), the discipline grew up along with the expansion of industrial capitalism. So one natural and, as it turned out, fruitful way to think about 'ordinary business' was to start with a self-interested individual interacting with many other self-interested individuals in a market setting, not by bilateral haggling but through the instrumentality of emerging market prices. From this came a great elaboration of ideas about supply, demand and price determination. That is the bread and butter of economics, and it fills the textbooks.

Some markets, however, have only a small number of participants, either naturally or because individuals learn to combine in cartels, trade associations, labor unions and so on. Sooner or later economists were bound to come upon the idea of strategic behavior, actions, and communications intended not so much to express individual preferences but to influence the behavior of other participants. The preferred method has been game theory, now all the rage in economics (represented in this book by the chapter by John Nash). One of the by-products has been careful attention to the way in which institutional arrangements and regulations affect the incentives that motivate decisions. A further natural extension is to political economy, a systematic attempt to include the making of economic policy as an integral part of an analytical description of the economic system. Economic events influence political actions, and political actions influence economic events.

There is another interesting pathway leading from the close study of individual markets toward much broader issues. Market economies have always been subject to pervasive *aggregative* movements in the form of irregular fluctuations, somewhat more regular business cycles, and variations in the rate of growth. Besides, the dominating circumstance facing the individual buyer or seller is often the alternation of good times and bad times. This has led to the development of a branch of economics – macroeconomics – devoted to the study of the aggregative behavior of market economies, and of course to the way in which aggregative behavior relates to microeconomic institutions and regularities. Many of the chapters in this book – those by Paul Krugman, Finn Kydland, Vernon Smith, Michael Spence – fall into this category. Because unemployment is such a pervasive and painful consequence of macroeconomic distress, the role of the labor market as the cause and consequence of aggregative fluctuations has come in for special attention (see the chapters by Peter Diamond and Dale Mortensen).

Macroeconomics tends to be a contentious part of the discipline, for at least two reasons: there is a lot at stake, and the underlying facts of the economy can change relatively quickly. For example, the world has just learned, all too obviously, that the extraordinary proliferation of financial activity in recent decades can have serious, even calamitous, consequences for the whole economy. Macroeconomics had not kept up adequately with this phenomenon, but we can be sure that it will pay more attention to it in the future. It is not an accident that today heads of the two important central banks, the European Central Bank and the US Federal Reserve System, as well as of several smaller ones, are trained economists.

The likelihood that the economy itself changes from time to time in functionally significant ways lends liveliness and excitement to economics. A critic once complained to John Maynard Keynes that he seemed to change his mind fairly often. There were even jokes about it. Keynes is said to have replied: 'When the facts change, I change my mind. What do you do, sir?' The large-scale financialization of economic activity was one such change. There have been others throughout history: the shift from agriculture to industry was one, the so-called demographic transition was another. It is possible that the proliferation of low-cost, easy-access information through the Internet will be yet another. If that turns out to be the case, some of the economics of individual markets will have to be rewritten. One of the standard assumptions has been that all participants share the same information, usually complete information, about prices, qualities, available alternatives and so on. More recently, much interesting and important work has examined the consequences of *asymmetric information* – for example, the likelihood that the seller of a good or service knows more about its characteristics than any potential buyer. It is no surprise that this changes the way a market works and the benefits it confers. Maybe the Internet will move the world closer to the classical assumption, but maybe not. That may depend on the economics of the Internet itself.

Some chapters in this book illustrate still other aspects of private and social life that can be analyzed using the tools of economics. William Sharpe reasons about Everyman's problem of providing an adequate income during the years of retirement, a problem that becomes more acute with increasing longevity. Oliver Williamson considers how the once-neglected costs of decision-making affect both the internal organization of firms and the structure of industry. My own contribution focuses on a particular class of goods – natural and environmental resources – which presents special problems, and slips over into discussing how a society *should* organize their use.

A mere dozen chapters by a dozen authors could not hope to cover the whole territory of economics. As it happens, there is no chapter on international trade, nor is there one on the special problems of poor and developing countries, nor on financial markets and their interaction with the 'real' economy, nor on taxation and the economics of the public sector more generally. These and others are all active branches of research and teaching. Economics really is everywhere.

There is something else about economics that a potential student should know because it is part of the atmosphere of the discipline as it is practiced in universities, think-tanks, financial institutions, business firms, and government offices. Most of what economics is about consists of prices and quantities, or (like incomes) can be expressed in terms of prices and quantities. These are naturally numerical objects, and they lend themselves to data collection and statistical analysis.

Recent decades have seen an enormous proliferation of large-scale data collection, mostly by government agencies, but also by private research organizations, including observations on the characteristics and behavior of individual persons and families. (To mention the most recent development, widespread credit card use and the growth of online purchasing have made it possible to collect immense bodies of data on individual retail transactions.) Many of the questions one would like to answer are themselves quantitative. How sensitively do purchases respond in prices, or do saving decisions respond to interest rates? How much time and money do families spend in caring for children or old people or disabled members? As a result, econometrics, the application of statistical methods in economic analysis, has become an essential part of the work of economists, and therefore of their training.

All that a book like this can do is to give a little taste of 'what economists do'. We know from recent history that, as our economies have evolved, they are capable of functioning well and badly. When they function badly, they can cause prolonged distress, inflicting harm on many passive victims who have done nothing to deserve it. In the aftermath of economic failure a lot of badly thought-out ideas circulate, many of them seeming to originate on some other planet. The fundamental goal of economics as a discipline is to bring organized reason and systematic observation to bear on both large and small economic problems (and to have some intellectual fun on the way).

Robert M. Solow
Lexington, Massachusetts
2013

Chapter 1
Paul R. Krugman

BIOGRAPHY

PAUL ROBIN KRUGMAN, USA

ECONOMICS, 2008

Paul Krugman is an economist known for his forthrightness on economic policy. He has criticized the Obama administration for not being 'forceful' enough or investing enough in the stimulus plan after the 2008 financial crisis. He had several run-ins with the George W. Bush administration and criticized the Reagan and Bush eras for policies that pandered to millionaires while creating the widest wealth gap in the USA since the 1920s. Despite this, he served as an economics advisor to President Ronald Reagan, albeit only for a year.

His Nobel Prize in Economics was awarded 'for his analysis of trade patterns and location of economic activity', which integrated the fields of international and regional economics into a new international trade and economic geography.

The traditional view of international trade was based on the notion that there is a technology-based caste system of nations. The lower caste has cheap labor and exports raw materials and food; the higher caste exports manufactured goods.

Increasingly, since World War II, globalization and urbanization have changed the face of international trade and blurred the distinctions of the 'caste' system, as electricity becomes more common (in urban areas, at least) and cheaper goods moving faster in larger quantities have raised lifestyle expectations in poorer areas.

In 1979, Krugman devised a new model to take these changes into account – an increasing spiral of more consumers demanding a varied supply of goods, being catered for by cheaper methods of mass production and distribution. As a result, small-scale production for a local market is replaced by large-scale production for the world market.

The new theory explains why worldwide trade is dominated by similar countries trading in similar products: a country may both export and import cars. Large-scale production – and 'free trade' – result in lower prices and a greater diversity of commodities.

Krugman's model, although initially developed for international trade, also demonstrates a change in economic geography. The 'caste' system now demarcates a high-tech urban core and a less developed 'periphery' as an increasingly larger share of the world population shifts to cities. A growing urban population with higher wages encourages large-scale production and a greater range of goods. Again, this creates a spiral of further migration to metropolises.

Paul Robin Krugman was born in February 1953 in Albany, New York. His paternal grandparents emigrated to the USA from Poland in 1922. He grew up in Nassau County and attributes his love of economics to Isaac Asimov, whose Foundation novels featured scientists saving civilization by studying 'psychohistory'. Krugman felt economics was the next best alternative.

Krugman attended John F. Kennedy High School in Bellmore, New York, before gaining his BA with honors from Yale University in 1974 and his PhD three years later from the Massachusetts Institute of Technology (MIT). In 1978 he created a monopolistically competitive trade model and later wrote: '[I] knew within a few hours that I had the key to my whole career in hand.'

He joined the faculty of MIT in 1979 and from 1982 to 1983 worked at the Reagan White House on the staff of the Council of Economic Advisers. He rejoined MIT as a full professor in 1984 and in 2000 relocated to Princeton University as Professor of Economics and International Affairs. He has also taught at Stanford, Yale, and the London School of Economics, where he is currently Centenary Professor. His membership on high-ranking economics panels, many international awards and list of publications are too lengthy for inclusion here, but he has been praised for making economics accessible and even exciting through his books, blogs, and New York Times *columns.*

Krugman is married and lives in Princeton, New Jersey.

Depressions are Different

To this day, you fairly often encounter definitions of economics something like this: 'Economics concerns itself with the allocation of scarce resources among competing ends.' Workers trading off income for leisure; consumers choosing between cheese and wine; governments trading off guns for butter: these are the stuff of many a textbook example. There is, we are told, no such thing as a free lunch.

And most of the time there isn't; most of the time scarcity and opportunity cost – the cost of passing up the next best choice when taking a decision – is what economics is largely about. But not always. Sometimes, there are depressions.

When the economy is in a depression, scarcity ceases to rule. Productive resources sit idle, so that it is possible to have more of some things without having less of others; free lunches are all around. As a result, all the usual rules of economics are stood on their head; we enter a looking-glass world in which virtue is vice and prudence is folly. Thrift hurts our future prospects; sound money makes us poorer.

Moreover, that's the kind of world we have been living in for the past several years, which means that it is a kind of world that students should understand.

WHAT IS A DEPRESSION?

We know, more or less, what defines a recession – it is a period in which most things in the economy are heading down. In many countries the rule is two consecutive quarters of declining real GDP, while in the United States it is a subjective judgment of an independent panel, but minor questions of timing aside – did the recession start in December or January, did it end in the summer or the fall? – it is not really a controversial subject.

The same cannot be said about depressions. Are they simply very bad recessions? Sometimes people do try to define depressions that way, offering arbitrary criteria such as a fall of 10 percent or more in output. But when we talk about the Great Depression we don't just mean the plunge from 1929 to 1933, we mean the whole period from 1929 to 1939 or 1940, a period that included episodes of growth – in fact, growth at 8 percent a year between 1933 and 1937 – as well as periods of decline. What made it the Great Depression, as opposed to just two recessions plus two recoveries, was the fact that national economies were clearly operating far below capacity the whole time, even when they were expanding – and the fact that there did not seem to be an easy way to get out of the trap.

That last point is crucial. Garden-variety slumps end fairly quickly, in large part because there is a simple technocratic answer: central banks cut interest rates, and the economy pops back up. But during the Great Depression those banks couldn't do that, because short-term rates – which are the rates conventional monetary policy affects most directly – were very close to zero, and could not go any lower. Hence the situation that John Maynard Keynes described and analyzed in his 1936 masterwork *The General Theory of Employment, Interest, and Money* (Keynes 1936), in which the economy remained 'in a chronic condition of subnormal activity for a considerable period without any marked tendency either towards recovery or towards complete collapse'. Japan entered that condition in the 1990s; America, Britain, and much of Europe joined it there in 2008.

So depressions should really be defined in functional terms: they are situations in which the economy is persistently below capacity but the usual medicine for that ailment, monetary expansion, is ineffective, because short-term interest rates are already near zero.

How do economies get into such situations? In the case of both Japan in the 1990s and the North Atlantic economies today, the story involved a large debt-financed real estate bubble that eventually burst, leaving both an overhang of excess construction and an overhang of debt, both of which exert a persistently depressing effect on the economy – sufficiently depressing that even a zero short-term interest rate isn't low enough. But one should not get too hung up on the details of the boom that preceded the slump.

Actually, that is a general caution. Ever since people began noticing the phenomenon of business cycles, there has been a strong tendency to cast them as morality plays – to lavish attention on the excesses of the boom and assume, at least implicitly, that the slump that follows is a necessary consequence. Yet there is no good reason to believe that this is true – in fact, as we will see in this chapter, there is every reason to believe that it is not true, that persistent slumps can and should be avoided, no matter what went on in the previous boom. And the habit of seeing economic ups and downs in moral terms can get in the way of the right policies.

So, to return to the main line of argument – a depression, I have asserted, is a situation in which the economy is operating persistently below capacity, and in which ordinary, technocratic policy cannot restore full employment. Now, let's look at the difference that such a situation makes to the usual rules of economics.

PARADOXES OF THRIFT AND FLEXIBILITY

In a depression, aggregate demand is inadequate. That is, the total quantity of goods and services that all the players in an economy – consumers, businesses, and governments – are willing to purchase are less than the total quantity of goods and services that producers would be willing to produce. So demand, not productive capacity, is what constrains output – and the trade-offs that economics textbook writers love to emphasize no longer apply.

Suppose, for example, that you would like to see the government build more infrastructure – new roads, bridges, rail tunnels under New York's Hudson River (that's a personal sore spot, in case you haven't guessed). Ordinarily we would say that doing this would require doing less of something else – either consumers must be persuaded to consume less, or the government spending would have to 'crowd out' private investment. If the economy is in a depression, however, no such trade-off is required: the tunnels may be built by workers who would otherwise be unemployed, using construction equipment that would otherwise have sat idle. If you ask where the funds to pay for this come from, well, they may be raised by selling government bonds – but this borrowing does not compete with other uses of funds, because the very act of spending government money raises income, some of that increased income is saved, and the spending therefore creates the savings that are used to buy those government bonds.

You may find this implausible; you may believe that large-scale government borrowing must surely drive up interest rates. If so, you have a lot of company: many prominent people, some of them believing that they know a lot about economics, insisted loudly back in 2009 that the large budget deficits that were already looming would lead to much higher interest rates. But they didn't. I'm writing this chapter more than three years after some of those debates, and the interest rate on long-term US government bonds is less than 2 percent. We are living in an economy to which the usual rules do not apply.

Nor is that all. Depression economics is marked by paradoxes, in which seemingly virtuous actions have perverse, harmful effects. Two paradoxes in particular stand out: the paradox of thrift, in which the attempt to save more actually leads to the nation as a whole saving less, and the less-well-known paradox of flexibility, in which the willingness of workers to protect their jobs by accepting lower wages actually reduces total employment.

On the paradox of thrift: for the economy as a whole, savings are always equal to investment, as a matter of accounting. So suppose that some group in the economy, say households, becomes more future-oriented, more willing to defer present gratification and save for the future. Ordinarily we would expect this willingness to translate into higher overall investment spending, so that the economy would indeed make more provision for the future – building more factories, server farms, and office buildings in order to raise future productivity.

It is important, however, to understand how that process is supposed to work. How does a decision by John Q. Public, in Ho-Ho-Kus, New Jersey, to spend less and save more persuade Google to expand the Googleplex in Mountain View, California? The standard answer is that it works through interest rates: higher desired savings translate into lower rates, which either directly reduce borrowing costs or indirectly lead to higher stock prices; either way, the cost of capital falls for corporations considering expansion, and the result is more investment.

Now think about what happens in a depression. Interest rates, or at least short-term rates, cannot fall because they are already at zero. So the transmission mechanism from desired savings to investment is broken.

Instead, when John Q. Public cuts his spending, the result is just a fall in total spending – the economy becomes more depressed. This, in turn, will reduce, not increase, the amount that corporations are willing to invest, since there is less reason to expand capacity. Yet it is still true that savings equal investment in the aggregate, which means that overall savings fall. Hence the paradox of thrift: an attempt by some people to save more ends up reducing saving by the economy as a whole.

What about the paradox of flexibility? We normally imagine that the way to get people to buy more of something is to cut its price. So if there are not enough jobs, aren't wage cuts the answer? Many people think so, and in fact many conservative historians assert that the Great Depression would have ended much sooner if the US President Franklin Roosevelt had not allowed unions to oppose wage cuts and win wage increases.

Even in normal times, however, the relationship between wages and employment doesn't work in the way many imagine. It is true that workers in a particular industry or company can save their jobs by taking wage cuts. That's because by reducing wages their labor and the products they produce are made cheaper in relation to the labor and products of other workers. When the overall level of wages falls, however, no one gains a relative advantage. If there is any positive effect on employment, it happens via interest rates. In practice, the way this works tends to be through policy at the central bank: lower wages mean lower inflation, which encourages the central bank to cut interest rates, leading to higher demand and hence higher employment.

In a depression, however, interest rates cannot be cut. So there is no channel through which lower wages can raise employment! And the likely effect of wages cuts is in fact to reduce employment.

Why? Debt. Recall that the overhang of debt is probably one major reason that we're in a depression right now. Some 80 years ago, the great American economist Irving Fisher explained how this works (Fisher 1933). When individuals have run up debts that are now considered excessive, these debtors end up being forced to slash spending in order to pay that debt. Meanwhile, creditors face no comparable pressure to spend more. So debt that is seen as excessive creates a 'deleveraging' environment in which overall spending is depressed, possibly depressed enough to cause a depression.

In such an environment, what happens if the level of wages falls? Prices and incomes fall too – but debt does not. So the real burden of debt rises, reinforcing the depressing effect of

debt on spending. This means that having 'flexible' labor markets, in which wages fall quickly in the face of unemployment,
is actually a bad thing under depression conditions.

As I said, then, depression economics is a looking-glass
world in which the usual rules do not apply, and where some
effects are completely reversed. What does this say about
policy?

FIGHTING DEPRESSION

A depression is, by definition – by *my* definition, anyway – a
situation in which the normal policy measures we take to fight
recessions, mainly interest rate cuts by the central bank, are
insufficient. Yet this does not mean that nothing can be done.
The key is to think differently.

Just to be clear, the advice that follows applies only when
the economy is in a depression, with interest rates up against
the lower bound. You sometimes find 'vulgar Keynesians'
who insist on applying depression logic even when the economy is not in a depression. But the species is actually fairly
rare; you are much more likely to encounter anti-Keynesians
who either do not realize or choose not to realize that policy analysis in a depression is very different from analysis
in normal times, and that advocating such things as deficit
spending at a time like this does not mean advocating them
everywhere and always.

So what are the policy implications? First of all, the story
surrounding the paradox of thrift tells us that any player in
the economy who decides to spend less inflicts damage on
everyone else, and on the future too. Conversely, a player who
increases spending is helping the economy in both the short
and the long run. And there is at least one player who can and
should take these effects into account: the government. In
other words, the analysis of depression makes an immediate

case for fiscal stimulus – for increases in government spending, or possibly for transfers and tax cuts that promote private spending.

Again, under depression conditions government borrowing doesn't crowd out private investment – on the contrary, it probably leads to higher private investment, because a stronger economy gives businesses more reason to expand.

But isn't it irresponsible to borrow and burden future generations with debt? Not when you're in a depression, when the benefit of borrowing is that it helps put unemployed resources to work. In fact, there is a good case to be made that penny-pinching when the economy is deeply depressed is harmful even in purely fiscal terms. A depressed economy leads to low business investment, which reduces future productive capacity; it also leads to high long-term unemployment, which degrades skills and attachment to the world of work, reducing the future labor force. The result is surely lower output even in the long run – and lower output means lower revenue. Economists who have done the arithmetic, most notably Lawrence Summers and J. Bradford DeLong (2012), find that for reasonable parameters fiscal expansion in depressions is actually good for long-term fiscal health, and austerity bad.

The case for fiscal expansion is not the only thing that emerges when you take depression economics seriously. Depressions also offer a good reason to seek and maintain some inflation – maybe 4 percent – in times when there isn't a depression.

Why? Borrowing and spending, economists believe, depend on the *real* rate of interest – the nominal interest rate minus expected inflation. Nominal rates cannot go below zero, but real rates can and do. And central banks would be able to achieve a lower real rate right now if we had come into the slump with an inflation rate of 4 percent rather than 2 percent. This is, by the way, by no means an outlandish argument; it has been advanced by, among others, Olivier Blanchard, the chief economist of the International Monetary Fund (Blanchard, Dell'Arricia, and Mauro 2010).

A more controversial proposal is that the central banks try to convince the public that there will be higher inflation in the future than there has been in the past. This would be tricky, because such a policy depends not on current action, but on making promises about action some distance into the future. This might or might not work. The point, however, is that at times like this it would be helpful if central banks had less, not more, of a reputation for maintaining price stability.

In any case, the broader point should be clear. In times of depression, the rules are different. Conventionally sound policy – balanced budgets, a firm commitment to price stability – helps to keep the economy depressed.

Once again, this is not normal. Most of the time we are not in a depression. But sometimes we are – and 2013, when this chapter was written, was one of those times.

REFERENCES

Blanchard, Olivier, Dell'Arricia, Giovanni, and Mauro, Paulo. 2010. Rethinking macroeconomic policy. International Monetary Fund Staff Position Note, 12 February. http://www.imf.org/external/pubs/ft/spn/2010/spn1003.pdf.

DeLong, J. Bradford, and Summers, Lawrence. 2012. Fiscal policy in a depressed economy. *Brookings Papers on Economic Activity* (Spring), 233–274.

Fisher, Irving. 1933. The debt-deflation theory of Great Depressions. *Econometrica* 1(4), 335–357.

Keynes, John Maynard. 1936. *The General Theory of Employment, Interest, and Money*. London: Macmillan.

Chapter 2
Vernon L. Smith

BIOGRAPHY

VERNON L. SMITH, USA

ECONOMICS, 2002

Economic research has traditionally relied on observations of real economies, with research revolving around a nominal 'homo oeconomicus' capable of rational decision-making and motivated by self-interest, leaving no room for laboratory-style experiments.

The 2002 Nobel Prize in Economics, however, was shared by two men who took a more academic approach to the subject. Daniel Kahneman integrated economic science with psychological research into human judgment and decision-making. Vernon Smith developed a variety of experimental methods, demonstrating the importance of alternative market institutions, and instigated 'wind-tunnel' tests of new market designs in the lab before putting them into practice. His work has established experiments as a vital tool in empirical economic analysis. As a result of their efforts, there is now a growing body of research devoted to modifying and testing economic assumptions, using data collected in the lab and psychological analysis.

Vernon Lomax Smith was born in Wichita, Kansas, on New Year's Day, 1927, in the years leading up to the Great Depression, and says he is a product of the strange circumstances of survival, and of successes built on tragedy: he is the only child from his mother's second marriage. She was widowed at the age of 22 when her railway fireman husband was killed in a train crash. Vernon has two older half-sisters.

The life insurance paid for a small farm, and Vernon attended the local rural one-room schoolhouse. In 1934 the family lost the farm and returned to the city, where Vernon attended Wichita North High School.

Not surprisingly, he started work young, first in a local soda shop and then, at 16, at the Boeing aircraft factory, testing gun turret systems for B-29 bombers. In 1944 he spent a year at Friend's University, a Quaker College, studying physics, chemistry, calculus, astronomy, and literature, to boost his knowledge to get into the California Institute of Technology.

His plan succeeded and in September 1945 he took the Santa Fe train to Los Angeles. He attended lectures by Linus Pauling, Robert Oppenheimer, and Bertrand Russell.

Smith started out in physics, but changed to his major, electrical engineering, and received his BSc in 1949. However, he had taken a course in economics and got hooked. He moved back to the University of Kansas where he received an MA in economics in 1952, before moving to Harvard to earn his PhD in 1955.

At Harvard, Smith witnessed Edward Chamberlin carry out classroom economic experiments and decided to adapt the technique in his first teaching post at Purdue University to explain microeconomics to students. In the process, he stumbled upon a vehicle for testing ideas inside and outside traditional economic theory. After further trials, Smith wrote about his experiments for the Journal of Political Economy, *1962; experimental articles followed in 1964, 1965, and 1967.*

He stayed at Purdue until 1967, also teaching one year at Stanford before moving to New England, first at Brown University in Rhode Island and then the University of Massachusetts (1968–1972). Smith was granted a fellowship at the Center for Advanced Study in Behavioral Sciences (1972–1973) and the post of distinguished scholar at Caltech (1973–1975). At Caltech he was persuaded to write up his experimental system in many formal papers, starting in 1976. By this time, he was based at the University of Arizona, and it was here that much of his Nobel research was conducted. In 2001 Smith left Arizona for George Mason University, Virginia, where he remains as research scholar. In 2008 he founded the Economic Science Institute at Chapman University in Orange, California, where he is currently Professor of Economics. He is the founder and president of the International Foundation for Research in Experimental Economics, a Member of the Board of Advisors for The Independent Institute, and a Senior Fellow at the Cato Institute in Washington DC.

Among other tributes, the Universidad Francisco Marroquín in Guatemala named its Vernon Smith Center for Experimental Economics Research in his honor, and he also inspired The Vernon Smith Prize for the Advancement of Austrian Economics.

Smith is married and has four children.

✳   ✳   ✳   ✳   ✳

Rethinking Economics:
A Classical Perspective

The Great Recession has a simple explanation: with abandon people widely violated the basic rules of what Adam Smith would have called 'propriety' in his first and much neglected book, *The Theory of Moral Sentiments* (1759 [1982]). The rule violations were stated crisply in Shakespeare's maxim in *Hamlet*:

Neither a borrower nor a lender be;
For loan oft loses both itself and friend,
And borrowing dulls the edge of husbandry.

Similarly, the sentiment from Adam Smith's second book (1776 [1981], p. 741):

being the managers rather of other people's money than of their own, it cannot well be expected, that they should watch over it with the same anxious vigilance with which … (they) … frequently watch over their own.

Shakespeare expresses a truth with a poet's flare for hyperbole, while Adam Smith is acidly commenting on a 'bubble'. And indeed in the USA the Great Recession was launched on the heels of the collapse of the massive housing-mortgage market bubble that began in 1997; by 2001 the median price of a home had already achieved its previous all-time (inflation adjusted) high established in 1989. Instead of moderating, prices continued their ascent, halting abruptly in 2006, and then collapsing. Excessive credit financing of new home expenditures had driven house prices far above any semblance of equilibrium relative to all other prices and income.

As I write toward the end of 2012, we still await solid signs of a housing recovery; stay tuned. We finish our fifth year since the recent economic downturn that began at the end of 2007. For a sobering perspective, I want to note that the Great Depression began *c*.1929; so, measured in Depression time, we are near the end of 1934 when output grew by 7.7 percent.

In monitoring the state of our economy with unusual interest since 2007, I have learned a great deal. So, surely, have all the recognized policy and economic experts in these matters: if your views and understanding are not changing, you almost certainly are not learning. This is why it could be said that: 'The curious task of economics is to demonstrate to men how little they really know about what they imagine they can design' (Hayek 1988, p. 76).[1]

---

[1] I knew little of Hayek's work until after finding that contemporary equilibrium economics was incapable of dealing with what I was learning from laboratory market experiments in the 1950s and 1960s, and I was launched on a broader search for better understanding. Similarly, I began studying Adam Smith (1759) after realizing that the two-person experimental game results we were getting in the 1980s could not be comprehended within the framework of game theory, but this last story is much beyond the scope of what I will write here (see Smith, 2008a, 2008b). I will say only that I felt it necessary to re-examine and rethink first principles. Most of my colleagues in experimental economics were, I think, automatons in changing only the utility function – supplementing 'own' with 'other' payoffs in a routine fix that allowed all findings to be superficially reconciled with theory. Results that had not been predicted were rescued ex post by refitting the model with the utility function that would have made it predictive.

WHY THE 'BUSINESS CYCLE' IS
THE CONSUMER HOUSING CYCLE

Yes, houses are a consumer good, albeit extraordinarily durable. You can rent (lease) one and pay for its services as you live
in it; or buy one, and pay for its future stream of services in
an upfront purchase. And what that means for most people
of modest means was expressed in the quotation above from
Adam Smith: most of the purchase price will be in the form
of other people's money (OPM) – in particular, bank money,
which, if extended beyond levels sustainable by income growth,
endangers all depositors, including those who rent and were in
no sense part of the problem.

If most people buy homes with mostly OPM, and home
prices fall as in 2007–9, then many will be living in homes
worth less than their mortgage principal. In 2012, over 22 percent of would-be US home owners lived in properties where
their mortgage exceeds the market worth of their homes. They
are in a balance-sheet crunch, a condition that is not incorporated into models that are based on goods and money flows.
Moreover, symmetrically, the banks holding the mortgages
have the same problem. The Great Recession is a direct consequence of a household–bank balance-sheet crunch. It is not
simply a 'wealth effect', a label (like 'liquidity trap') that carries
no integrity of meaning or implications. For large numbers of
people their wealth *is* their home equity, and it is negative –
a black hole that permeates their dark outlook as they pay
down debt and gradually reboot their damaged balance sheets.
It carries a crippling burden of consequences because of the
fundamental behavioral asymmetry between gains and losses:
'We suffer more … when we fall from a better to a worse situation, than we ever enjoy when we rise from a worse to a better.
Security, therefore, is the first and the principal object of prudence … It is rather cautious than enterprising, and more anxious to preserve the advantages which we already possess, than

forward to prompt us to the acquisition of still greater advantages' (Smith 1759 [1982], p. 213). This continuing burden is why foreclosure in which both the bank and the household take their shared balance-sheet hits can actually be liberating for both, cruel as it appears at the time.[2]

Extensive balance-sheet damage lingers on today in the banks, and is marked by the observation that the equity shares of Bank of America, and of Citibank, two of the largest, are selling for half of their respective book values; this tells you vividly how skeptical are investors of how these banks are treating the book value of their assets.[3]

My major theme here is that in the long view it turns out that the typical recession is closely related to expenditures on new homes, exactly as in the Great Recession, but the ups and downs in housing – and their impact on the economy – are

---

[2] In 1934, my parents lost our Kansas farm to the bank in foreclosure.

[3] As long as you are meeting your payments on a mortgage the bank carries the loan at its full principal value, although the market would deeply discount the loan if the underlying collateral value of the home is less than the mortgage principal. The bank, recognizing these conditions, cannot entirely hide this condition under the bookkeeping rug: rather it is revealed in their reluctance to make new net loan commitments until their balance sheet is stronger. In 2012 bank revenue growth was still negative; the flow of new mortgage loans was negative – principal reduction exceeds new loans. Since 2008 the failure (bankruptcy) of over 400 small to medium-sized banks has been supervised by the Federal Deposit Insurance Corporation (FDIC), with the assets of the failed banks being sold at discounts representing current market value to survivors whose balance sheets have been strengthened. This is what bankruptcy is for: quickly if not painlessly to repair damaged balance sheets so that the world's work can return to normal. Insofar as the giant banks have been sheltered from being put through that wringer, the economy suffers, and the world's work is not getting done.

not usually on such an immense scale. The consistent connection between housing and the state of the economy is the most closely guarded secret in macroeconomic analysis and policy. When my colleague Steven Gjerstad and I began our studies of the last 14 recessions we started with the Great Recession. Having digested its background and housing origins, and the magnitude of the collapse, we thought that it was probably an anomaly. After revisiting the Great Depression and the 12 intervening recessions, we discovered unexpectedly and to our surprise that except for its severity the Great Recession was not anomalous (see Gjerstad and Smith 2009a, 2009b).

This learning is visually conveyed in a single chart plotting expenditures on housing as a percentage of GDP over the last 14 US recessions. Declines in this series for three years ominously preceded the Great Depression; declines for almost two years ushered in the Great Recession, 2007–8. These two Great Depressions were unusual, but what is usual about the intervening, less dramatic, recessions is that almost all of them (11 of the 14) were preceded by downturns in housing. There are a few that constitute false positives (or negatives) as predictors of recession, but each exception – for example, the post-World War II conversion, 1946, the delay effect of the Korean War, and the Vietnam War – can be fully understood by examining their special circumstances (see Gjerstad and Smith 2012).

So far I have referred only to housing as a quite consistent leading indicator of downturns – consistent enough that if you were on the US Federal Reserve Board you might want to do more than to just watch it.[4] But what can be said about the

---

[4] Here is a refreshingly candid admission of learning: 'Although I was concerned about the potential fallout from a collapse of the housing market, I think that it is fair to say that these costs have turned out to be much greater than I and many other observers

Figure 2.1   Expenditures on new single-family and multi-family housing units as a percentage of GDP, 1920–2010 (the shaded bars mark the last 14 recessions)

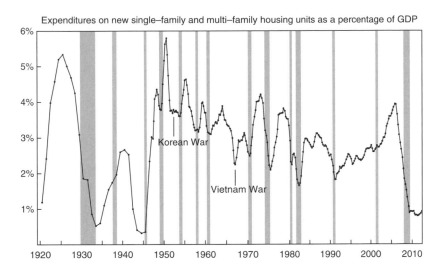

Expenditures on new single–family and multi–family housing units as a percentage of GDP

Source: Gjerstad and Smith 2012: ch.5, fig. 1

relation of housing expenditures to upturns in the economy? The empirical answer is very simply stated without any need for grasping at qualifications: if there is no recovery in housing, there is no sustained recovery in the economy. The Great Recession may be an exception, but its aftermath is not yet over. The proof of the proposition is to look at the figure; in the white spaces immediately after each recession, housing is increasing as a share of GDP.

---

imagined. In particular, I and other observers underestimated the potential for house prices to decline substantially, the degree to which such a decline would create difficulties for homeowners, and, most important, the vulnerability of the broader financial system to these events.' Donald L. Kohn, Vice Chairman, Board of Governors of the Federal Reserve System (Kohn 2008, p. 33).

WHO ARE WE TO BLAME FOR THE
GREAT RECESSION?

Essentially everyone is to blame, yet no one in particular. The blamable include: home buyers, real estate agents, lenders, mortgage originators, banks, 'financial innovation' (mortgage-backed securities – we had them in the form of mortgage bonds in the 1920s – and credit default swaps, euphemistically called 'insurance', etc.), deregulators, regulators, finance ministers, politicians, central bankers, and so on. It has been said: 'We have met the enemy, and he is us!' (Smith 2007). Everyone was caught up in myopically self-reinforcing expectations of rising prices.

In 2008, politicos as diverse as Alan Blinder, John McCain, and Hillary Clinton all recognized publicly that the household–bank balance-sheet crunch was immobilizing both normal household demand and normal bank lending, and should be addressed – as it had been addressed in the Great Depression.[5] (The Home Owners' Loan Corporation (HOLC), established in 1933, purchased one million home mortgages and reissued them to reflect the current market worth of the homes, reducing principal owed to the new market value. In the current crisis, I much preferred recapitalizing the banks

---

[5] Alan Blinder (2008), long-time advisor to leading Democrats, articulated the case for buying up negative-equity mortgages and replacing them with new market-based mortgages. The proposal was reported as being favored by Democratic Senator Chris Dodd. Hillary Clinton (2008) also proposed reviving the Home Owners' Loan Corporation (HOLC); but as an erstwhile Democratic presidential contestant her views here seemed to have little influence on Obama (http://online.wsj.com/article/SB122230767702474045.html). Presidential candidate John McCain also announced support for such a plan in the second presidential debate. See 'McCain Announces $300 Billion Homeownership Plan'. in 'WSJ Blogs, Washington Wire', *Wall Street Journal*, 7 October 2008 (http://blogs.wsj.com/washwire/2008/10/07/mccain-announces-homeownership-resurgence-plan/).

to do it, as part of their bankruptcy, but reviving the taxpayer-funded HOLC was far better, I believed, than the taxpayer-funded Bush/Obama stimulus.) Did these proposals lead to a strong and resolute bipartisan consensus under Obama? No, although Bill Clinton had no difficulty in getting such a consensus to eliminate the capital gains tax on your house of up to half a million US dollars back in 1997! We humans are so constituted that we can only get a consensus on actions that we think are good news (or bad news) for almost everyone. This was recognized in the well-known first-century parable, which ends: 'Let he who has not sinned cast the first stone.'

NEITHER MONETARY POLICY NOR FISCAL STIMULUS ARE EFFECTIVE IN BALANCE-SHEET CRISES

Think of it this way: it appears that in both of the two Great Depressions of the last 80 years too many of the financial decision nodes sported negative-equity balances – liabilities exceeded the market value of assets pledged against them. What that means is that the flow of money (and the reverse flow of goods and services) through these nodes is disrupted by comparison with the state in which equity is positive almost everywhere. A balance sheet in negative equity at a decision node is analogous to a partially empty tank connected to the node: some of the flow through the node is diverted to filling up the tank – restoring the node's equity position.

So, monetary policy is ineffective as a stimulus, although I think, and it is certainly plausible, that Ben Bernanke (chairman of the US Federal Reserve Board) stemmed the occurrence of an even worse calamity (I can't say 'prevented').[6]

---

[6] Iceland followed the 'worst' route. Their GDP fell far more than in the United States, but from its low it is growing at a 5.5 percent rate in the five quarters of its recovery (see Gjerstad and Smith 2012).

We are living through times that are entirely different to any encountered in the past. As I see it, the US Federal Reserve thoroughly tested the Friedman-Schwartz (1963) hypothesis that the Great Depression had been 'caused' by the failure of the US central bank to provide adequate liquidity to the financial system. The test was initiated on 10 August 2007 and continued through September 2008, with ever-increasing 'liquidity enhancement'. This action failed to live up to its expectations, because the banks had a solvency problem, not merely a liquidity problem. So, the Federal Reserve moved to lift about $1.3 trillion of junky assets off the balance sheets of various banking institutions in the last quarter of 2008. Even so, as indicated above, two of the largest banks are yet (2012) to return to normal equity levels. There is still some hefty junk out there.

My hypothesis is that in 1930, the banks also had an insolvency problem, and the provision of liquidity alone would not have prevented a major downturn. I believe that the Great Recession will lead to a re-evaluation of the Great Depression, based on a broader understanding of crises, and of Friedman-Schwartz, that either disproves this hypothesis or fails to do so.

Moreover, fiscal stimulus is ineffective for the same reason that monetary ease is ineffective: too many nodes experience income flows that are leaking into their negative equity tanks. The government writes checks to people (as in the Bush stimulus) and many use it to pay down debt, or save, and some is spent at Wal-Mart where it goes to China for goods.[7] China

---

Austerity was unavoidable in Iceland, where the currency tubed but exports responded, balance-sheet restoration began, and the economy is not mired in disequilibrium like Ireland, Greece, and Spain, which are all handcuffed to the euro. Similarly, in the 1930s, recovery was initiated sequentially as one country after another went off gold.

[7] In terms of macro flow models it can be said that the marginal propensity to consume had decreased and the government spending multiplier was closer to 1.0 than normal. That was indeed part of

then recycles it into US Treasury debt issued to finance the government's expenditures. The Bush/Obama stimulus did not address the need to reboot household–bank balance sheets.

The hope that fiscal stimulus can work where monetary stimulus cannot, derives from the coincidence (and argument) that we did not really emerge from the Great Depression until the 1940s with the increase in government wartime spending.[8] But by 1940 we had experienced a decade of balance-sheet repair – bankruptcies, foreclosures, deleveraging, the HOLC. There is no evidence that the same fiscal stimulus would have been effective in 1930 when balance sheets were badly damaged.

The last half of the 20th century nurtured the belief that we had learned enough about monetary and fiscal policy to prevent crises comparable to the Great Depression from ever plaguing us again. That belief has been brutally shot down. We have confidently believed that we knew more than in fact we have been able to demonstrate that we know; our beliefs were false and our pretense has been exposed. We need to find solutions, not blame, as there is more than enough blame to go around.

REFERENCES

Blinder, A. 2008. From the new deal, a way out of a mess. *New York Times*, 24 February. http://www.nytimes.com/2008/02/24/business/24view.html.

---

the story of what happens to the normal income and spending flows in balance-sheet recessions; another part was that the stimulus brought a surge in US imports relative to exports after the second quarter of 2009, further dampening any potential domestic effects.
[8] I first heard this argument 60 years ago in Alvin Hansen's two graduate classes (Business Cycles and Monetary Theory) at Harvard University, 1952–3.

Clinton, Hillary. 2008. Let's keep people in their homes. *Wall Street Journal,* 15 September. http://online.wsj.com/article/SB122230767702474045.html.

Friedman, Milton, and Jacobson Schwartz, Anna. 1963. *A Monetary History of the United States, 1867–1960.* Princeton: Princeton University Press.

Gjerstad, Steven, and Smith, Vernon L. 2009a. From bubble to depression? *Wall Street Journal,* 6 April, p. A15.

Gjerstad, Steven, and Smith, Vernon L. 2009b. Monetary policy, credit extension, and housing bubbles: 2008 and 1929. *Critical Review,* 2–3, 269–300.

Gjerstad, Steven, and Smith, Vernon L. 2012. At home in the Great Recession. In *The 4 Percent Solution,* ed. B. Miniter. Dallas: Crown Press.

Hayek, F. A. 1988. *The Fatal Conceit.* Chicago: University of Chicago Press.

Kohn, D. L. 2008. Monetary policy and asset prices revisited. Speech at the Cato Institute 26th Monetary Policy Conference, Washington D.C., 19 November. Published 2009, *Cato Journal,* 29(1): 31–44.

Smith, Adam. 1759 [1982]. *The Theory of Moral Sentiments.* Indianapolis: Liberty Fund.

Smith, Adam. 1776 [1981]. *An Inquiry into the Nature and Causes of the Wealth of Nations,* vol. 2. Indianapolis: Liberty Fund.

Smith, Vernon L. 2007. We have met the enemy, and he is us. *AEI-Brookings,* Paper 07-32, 20 December.

Smith, Vernon L. 2008a. Theory and experiment: what are the questions? *Journal of Economic Behavior and Organization* 73, pp. 3–15.

Smith, Vernon L. 2008b. What would Adam Smith say? *Journal of Economic Behavior and Organization* 73, pp. 83–86.

Chapter 3
Peter A. Diamond

BIOGRAPHY

PETER A. DIAMOND, USA

ECONOMICS, 2010

In April 2010, with the USA facing a continuing housing and jobs crisis, President Obama nominated three new members to the Board of Governors of the Federal Reserve. Two of the nominees were accepted by the US Senate, but Republicans, led by Alabama Senator Richard Shelby, blocked the appointment of Peter Diamond. Republicans claimed that Diamond lacked experience in conducting monetary policy and in crisis management.

Six months after Diamond's nomination came the announcement of the 2010 Nobel in Economics award to him, shared with Dale Mortensen and Christopher Pissarides, 'for their analysis of markets with search frictions'. The three Laureates have formulated a theoretical framework for search markets, such as the job market, in which buyers and sellers do not always make contact with one another immediately. Since the search process requires time and resources, it creates frictions in the market. Their models help explain how unemployment, job vacancies, and wages are affected by economic regulations, and how they could help guide government to find the best solution. Search theory applies to many other areas, in particular the housing market, monetary theory, public economics, financial economics, regional economics, and family economics.

The prize committee also cited Diamond's work on frictions in markets in a broader sense, including his work on missing markets, overlapping generations, and the more 'traditional' theory of public finance.

Of the Nobel Prize, Senator Shelby said the Royal Swedish Academy 'does not determine who is qualified to serve' on the Federal Board. In a 6 June 2011 op-ed in the New York Times, Diamond withdrew his nomination and responded to some of the statements made about him. He pointed out that understanding the labor market was critical for devising an effective monetary policy, and that crisis prevention, not just crisis management, was central for the Federal Reserve. Of real relevance was his work on the labor market, which was central to his Nobel Prize, and his work on capital markets, which was cited by the Nobel Committee as well.

Peter Arthur Diamond was born in New York City in April 1940. After graduating summa cum laude in mathematics from Yale

University in 1960, he received his PhD from the Massachusetts Institute of Technology in 1963.

He taught at the University of California, Berkeley from 1963 to 1966 before returning to MIT as an associate professor in 1966, serving as head of the Department of Economics 1985–1986, and being named an Institute Professor (an honorific title at MIT) in 1997.

He wrote his first major paper in 1965 and at the age of 28 was elected a Fellow, and later served as President, of the Econometric Society. He has also served as President of the American Economic Association, is a Fellow of the American Academy of Arts and Sciences, a member of the National Academy of Sciences, and in 1988 helped found the National Academy of Social Insurance. He is known for his analysis of US social security policy and his work as an advisor to the Advisory Council on Social Security in the late 1980s and 1990s.

Diamond is married and has two children.

Employment and Unemployment

In the teaching of how an economy works, a key role is played
by the abstraction of a 'market'. Another word for an abstraction is a model. A model of a market is written in terms of
the demand for a particular good, the supply of the good, and
a price that clears the market – the price that results in the
number of items that people want to buy at that price equal
to the number of items that people want to sell at that price.
As an example, think about snow shovels in winter, which are
stocked by stores waiting to sell them and are sought by households. The abstraction, the model, is only approximate – not
every shovel that is stocked will be sold and not every family looking for a shovel will find one quickly. And the model
does not address the more complex question of who buys from
which store. Nevertheless, the model captures the idea that, for
many goods, most of the time, sales do roughly match both
what is stocked and what is sought for purchase, despite a total
absence of any central planning. Some markets, like the sea-
sonal clothing market, for instance, work rather differently
as only some items are sold during the prime season, some
are sold at reduced prices afterwards, and, as fashions change,
some items are not sold at all.

Any model is a simplification of reality and so omits elements
that are important for some issues even though they are unimportant for other issues. So, a helpful model can help guide
our intuition of some of what happens when circumstances
change, even though it is not helpful about other elements of
change. For example, if the cost of producing shovels increases,
the price will tend to go up. If there is a forecast of a bad winter,
demand will go up, and again, the price will tend to go up.

I have used the mealy-mouthed expression 'tend to go up' to reflect the idea that there is a force that is moving the price in that direction, but other factors may also impact on the price, possibly in the opposite direction. If we gather data on sales achieved under different circumstances over a period of time, we can even estimate how much the price and quantity sold tend to change when circumstances change.

Expanding the range of applications, we can consider that prices do not always clear markets. The government might set a limit on the price that can be charged that is below the price that would clear the market. Then, stores will stock out and some people will not be able to buy at the going price. Or, with news that a big storm is coming, many people may rush out to buy shovels, some stores may not raise their prices (to preserve the goodwill of customers), the stores will stock out and again some people will not be able to buy at the going price. In this type of setting, when the price does not clear the market, either there is leftover supply or there are disappointed would-be buyers.

In an important respect, the labor market is different. In the US economy, millions of workers are hired each month. And a roughly similar number leave their jobs, some by quitting, some by being discharged, and some by retiring. The change in the number employed is the relatively small difference between the large number of those hired and the large number of those leaving their jobs. For example, it is estimated that in November 2011, 4.132 million workers were hired, while 3.986 million separated from their jobs. The change in the number of filled jobs was 146,000 (equal to 4.132 million minus 3.986 million). Yet all the time there are workers seeking jobs who do not yet have one – the unemployed. And there are firms that are trying to hire workers, but have not yet succeeded – unfilled job openings, or vacancies. In the simple market model described above, there can be an excess demand or an excess supply, but not both at the same time. The US labor market is very dynamic and there is both excess demand and excess supply at the same time, all of the time.

So we can ask what makes the market for workers different from the market for shovels. And we can ask what models might be more informative for thinking about the labor market.

Firms manufacture and sell a variety of different models of shovels. And different firms produce somewhat different lines of shovels. For the purposes of our questions, we are not interested in who ends up with which shovel or who bought at which store (although the stores and the manufacturers are very interested in these questions). When it comes to workers and jobs, there are lots of reasons to care about who gets which job, and to care about the impact of the business cycle on the number of people employed and the number unemployed, and the number who have dropped out of the labor market because they are discouraged about their employment prospects. And we care a great deal about what the government can do through monetary and fiscal policy to limit the numbers of people who are unable to find suitable jobs.

Current thinking about these issues recognizes that a model with simultaneous unemployment and vacancies is a better starting place for policy analysis than the simple model that has only excess demand or excess supply. Such modeling with both unemployment and vacancies is referred to as search theory, reflecting the fact that it usually takes time and effort for workers to locate new jobs and for firms to locate new workers. We can relate the numbers of new hires to the numbers of job seekers and of job openings. This moves the thinking beyond a focus on how and why the wage does not adjust to clear the labor market. The inadequacy of that way of thinking, the need for recognition of additional factors, was at the heart of the innovative analysis of John Maynard Keynes in his famous 1936 book, *The General Theory of Employment, Interest and Money*. Contrasting his approach with that of standard earlier analysis, referred to as classical thinking, Keynes wrote: 'For the Classical Theory has been accustomed to rest the supposedly self-adjusting character of the economic system on an assumed fluidity of money-wages; and, when there is rigidity, to lay on this rigidity the blame of maladjustment' (p. 257). Unfortunately, there are still analysts who focus too narrowly on wage adjustment, on 'sticky wages', wages that do not adjust quickly, while assuming that more rapid adjustment would be sufficient to eliminate cyclical unemployment, paying too little attention to other aspects of the functioning of the economy.

That is, Keynes argued that to understand the high unemployment of the Great Depression of the 1930s, and so to have a better basis for economic policy, while there is a role for how wages evolve when there is much unemployment, analysis also has to consider more than just that. In Keynes's view, a central role is played by how much people are prepared to spend on consumption and on new investment when there is high unemployment, referred to as effective demand. And the same perspective holds for the Great Recession we are experiencing currently.

To proceed, let's contrast the numbers in the USA for November 2011 with those from four years earlier, just before the Great Recession had set in. Already, total employment was growing slowly. In November 2007, 4.657 million workers were hired, while 4.599 million separated from their jobs. The change in the number of filled jobs was only 58,000 (equal to 4.657 million minus 4.599). As can be seen in Figure 3.1, hires and separations were both much higher in 2007, although the change in total employment was actually lower. Behind the large number of hires was a large number of job openings. Hires and separations are measured by asking a large sample of firms how many people were added to their payrolls the previous month, and how many people left their payroll. Unlike these measures based on the entire month, the number of job openings was just the number at a single point in the month. But this reflects

Figure 3.1   Job openings and labor turnover

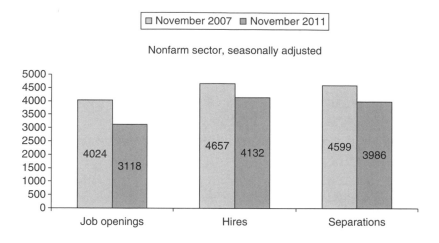

Note: All numbers are in thousands
Sources: BLS News Release, JOLTS, 7 February 2012; BLS News
Release, JOLTS, 12 February 2008

the numbers during the month, as jobs typically get filled relatively quickly and people get hired throughout the month. In
November 2007, the estimated number of job openings was
4.024 million, while in November 2011, the number was nearly
25 percent lower, at 3.118 million. With many more unemployed workers, job openings were filled more quickly so the
ratio of hires to job openings was somewhat higher in 2011 –
1.33 rather than 1.16.

The central policy issue for the sorry state of the economy
in 2011 is this low number of job openings. Job openings are
created when firms think it profitable to hire more workers
in order to have more ability to sell, and expect to succeed in
making higher sales. Job openings also occur when workers
quit for better job opportunities, leaving behind a vacant position that it is profitable to fill. When the job opportunities are
not so good, there are fewer quits – there were 22 percent fewer
quits in November 2011 than in November 2007.

In a normal recession, the government encourages more job openings through monetary policy. By lowering the interest rate, the central bank encourages both consumption spending and investment spending by making it less expensive to borrow. The increased level of effective demand encourages firms to produce more because they anticipate being able to sell more. When they hire more workers, and pay them, these workers spend more, helping sales and so encouraging more hires. This virtuous circle, referred to as a multiplier effect, helps to lessen the depth of a recession and helps to pull the economy back toward a healthier state.

In the Great Recession the US central bank, the US Federal Reserve System, lowered interest rates as far as they could go – as the interest rate cannot go negative. And the Federal Reserve System engaged in non-standard actions (buying assets) to further encourage economic growth. But these steps have not been enough, given how deep the recession has been and the lingering effects of the weakness in the banking system and of the large drop in prices of homes and commercial real estate. To supplement monetary policy, the US government has engaged in fiscal policy: temporarily lowering taxes, increasing spending, and providing funds to states to lower the extent to which states cut spending in response to the large drop in state tax revenues. As the poor state of the economy has gone on longer than was anticipated at the start, many of these fiscal measures have run their course, and we should be thinking of further steps to help the economy to grow more rapidly, to raise the level of employment and profitability.

Thinking through how the economy works, building models, and seeing how the models fit with empirical facts, play a critical role in designing economic policies that keep an eye on the best estimates of how they will affect the economy. The development of models for thinking about the labor market in terms of the flows of hires and separations was the central basis for the Nobel Memorial Prize that I shared with Dale Mortensen and Christopher Pissarides in 2010. Information about this work and that of other economics prize winners, and about the ceremonies in Stockholm, can be found on the Nobel Prize website, http://www.nobelprize.org/nobel_prizes/ economics/laureates/.

Chapter 4
Dale T. Mortensen

BIOGRAPHY

DALE T. MORTENSEN, USA

ECONOMICS, 2010

In a timely manner, the Nobel Prize in Economics for 2010 was awarded to three economists whose work focuses on a problem that could be faced at any time, but most acutely during a recession.

'Search frictions' in a market – notably areas such as employment and housing – affect both buyers and sellers as each seeks

their ideal situations. You might have found a lovely house, for example, but is it in the right location? Or you may be seeking staff with a certain set of skills that you can also afford to employ, but is it worth opening a high-tech factory in the countryside if all the workers with the skills you require are in the city?

The time and effort spent in search can erode confidence over time, particularly for those seeking work. How long does one search before giving up, staying put, accepting a lesser role or getting stuck in an unemployment rut?

Peter Diamond, Dale Mortensen, and Christopher Pissarides all made a study of these 'frictions', with a view to how economic policy may best be tailored to suit the demands of the marketplace.

One conclusion is that unemployment benefits have to be carefully pitched – too high and the unemployed have less incentive to work; too low and they can slide into a poverty trap and become disengaged with the workforce.

As is often the case in economics, Mortensen has spent decades studying what appears to be common sense. But he has extended his research to study labor turnover and reallocation at a macroeconomic level, as well as research and development, and personal relationships. His assessment, that friction is equivalent to the random arrival of trading partners, is now the accepted technique for analysis of labor markets and the effects of employment policy.

Robert Coen, Professor Emeritus of Economics at Northwestern University, Evanston, Illinois, explained: 'By advancing models of how markets actually work, Mortensen lays the groundwork for systematic assessments of the impacts of economic policies on market performance – for example, on how unemployment benefits or employment subsidies affect unemployment and the allocation of labor.'

Dale Thomas Mortensen was born in February, 1939, in Enterprise, Oregon. He received his BA in Economics from Willamette University in Salem, Oregon, and his PhD from Carnegie Mellon University in Pittsburgh, Pennsylvania. He joined the faculty of Northwestern University in 1965, where he is now the Ida C. Cook Professor of Economics. Among other prestigious roles and awards he was the Niels Bohr Visiting Professor of Economics and Management at Aarhus University, Denmark, from 2006 to 2010, and a building there has been named in his honor. He is also a Northwestern Board of Trustees Professor.

Mortensen is married and has two children.

Unemployment During and After the Great Recession

After the collapse of the global financial firm of Lehman Brothers in September 2008, the United States and Europe experienced their most severe financial market panic and banking crisis since the beginning of the Great Depression. Although the US Treasury Department and the Federal Reserve System took immediate action in an attempt to prevent a complete meltdown of financial markets, it became clear that the usual tools at hand were insufficient for the purpose. In response, on 3 October President Bush signed a $700 billion bill known as the Troubled Asset Relief Program (TARP), designed to shore up the banking system, and financial markets more generally. On the same day, the Labor Department's Bureau of Labor Statistics reported the loss of some 159,000 jobs in the previous month, the largest monthly decline in five years.

During the next two years, the Dow Jones Industrial Average, Nasdaq Composite, and S&P 500 index all experienced declines of greater than 20 percent from their peaks in late 2007. The estimates of the decline in the value of residential housing were even greater, about 40 percent on average. Although the banking system eventually stabilized, the effects of the crisis and the decline in the value of household assets on employment and production of goods and services continued. During this period, now known as the Great Recession, the USA experienced the largest drop in employment since World War II. Employment had started to decline already by December 2007. The number of workers employed fell from a high of 138 million that month to 129 million two years later, while the unemployment rate rose by five percentage points to just over 10 percent of the labor force. As of the end of 2011, employment had only returned to 132 million people, while the unemployment rate fell to 8.5 percent. As the labor force grows at about 1 percent per year, current employment is at least 7 million below trend, in spite of the 2009 fiscal stimulus bill passed and signed by President Obama in February that pumped 787 billion federal dollars into the economy during the following two years.

Although the timing of the Great Recession was not fully anticipated, its causes are clear. After a long run-up in the prices of residential housing, the price bubble burst. As the value of residential housing fell for the first time in over 70 years, so did the value of the mortgage loans secured by these assets. Questionable practices associated with extending the loans that fueled the bubble added to the problems, as well as the introduction of complicated, not-well-understood financial instruments used to sell these mortgages to investors. These complications, together with a banking system that had inadequate reserves to deal with the risks taken, led to the crisis – one that required unprecedented actions by the US federal government and the nation's central bank, the Federal Reserve.

But why did all these financial developments affect the labor market? What is the connection between a banking crisis and unemployment? The answers to these questions are not well understood by economists, in part because financial crises are relatively rare.[1] Indeed, the 2008–9 recession was the only one caused by such a crisis since World War II. In other words, there simply is not that much history to guide us.

---

[1] A notable study of the history of financial crises over the past eight hundred years is summarized in the recent book by Carmen M. Reinhart and Kenneth S. Rogoff (2009), *This Time It's Different: Eight Centuries of Financial Folly* (Princeton, NJ: Princeton University Press).

Figure 4.1   Unemployment rate, 1948–2010

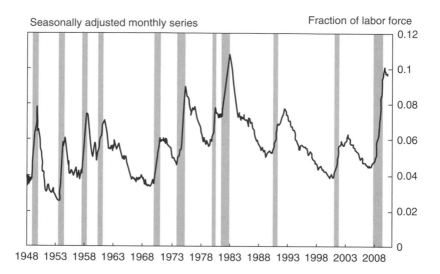

Source: Bureau of Labor Statistics

Less severe recessions with other causes are not uncommon. All of these events have featured considerable fluctuation in the fraction of workers seeking jobs, those defined by official statistics as unemployed. The official government unemployment series for the post-World War II period is presented in Figure 4.1 (time in years is plotted along the horizontal axis and the unemployment rate is indicated on the vertical axis; the shaded areas represent recession periods as determined by a committee of the National Bureau of Economic Research).[2] As indicated in Figure 4.1, there have been 11 recessions in the 1948–2010 time period, one every five to six years. Relative to a long-term average value of roughly six percentage points, the unemployment rate nearly doubled in the two worst recessions, those of 1983 and 2008, and then fell by almost half during some of the boom periods.

---

[2] For details, see http://www.nber.org/cycles/sept2010.html.

What is the unemployment rate, why is it important, and what does it measure? The answer to this last question is complicated, as suggested by the following exchange facetiously attributed to the famous but long-dead comic pair, Abbott and Costello:

COSTELLO: I want to talk about the unemployment rate in America.

ABBOTT: Good subject. Terrible times. It's about 9 percent.

COSTELLO: That many people are out of work?

ABBOTT: No that's 16 percent.

COSTELLO: You just said 9 percent.

ABBOTT: Nine percent unemployed.

COSTELLO: Right, 9 percent out of work.

ABBOTT: No that's 16 percent.

COSTELLO: Okay so it's 16 percent unemployed.

ABBOTT: No that's 9 percent.

COSTELLO: Wait a minute. Is it 9 percent or 16 percent?

ABBOTT: 9 percent are unemployed; 16 percent are out of work.

COSTELLO: If you're out of work you're unemployed.

ABBOTT: No you can't count the 'out of work' as the unemployed. You have to look for work to be unemployed.

COSTELLO: But … they're out of work!

Source: The Economics of Abbott and Costello posted in the online edition of *The Huffington Post*, 28th November 2011 © Barry Levinson, 2011.

Abbott is right; the official measure of unemployment is the fraction of the labor force who have been actively seeking a job, while the labor force is the sum of the unemployed so defined plus the employed. The measure does not include those who want a job but have stopped looking, or those who wish to work more hours but can only find part-time employment. Nevertheless, the data for all of these measures are

Figure 4.2   Comparison of BLS alternative national unemployment rates

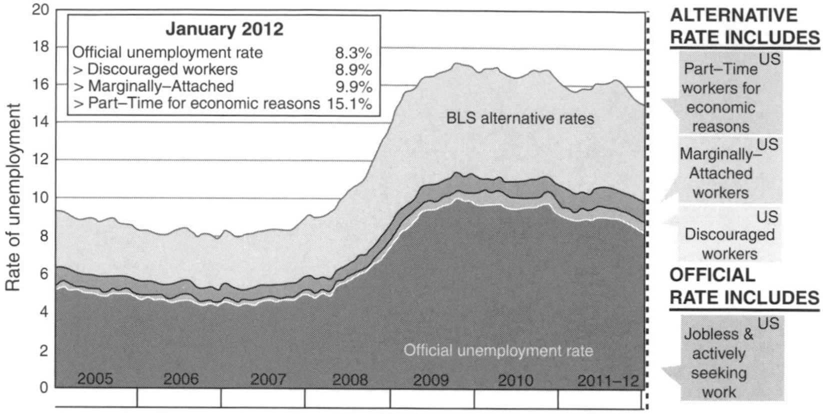

January 2012	
Official unemployment rate	8.3%
> Discouraged workers	8.9%
> Marginally–Attached	9.9%
> Part–Time for economic reasons	15.1%

Source: Bureau of Labor Statistics

collected in the monthly Census of Population Survey (CPS) of about 60,000 US households conducted by the US Census Bureau. The various unemployment measures over the last several years are illustrated in Figure 4.2.[3] The fact that the official unemployment rate was 8.3 percent of the labor force in January 2011, but a total of 15.5 percent were either jobless but desired employment, or wished to work full-time, explains Costello's confusion. However, as the graph in Figure 4.2 illustrates, the narrow official measure of unemployment and the broader definition generally move closely together over the business cycle and so reflect similar forces at work in the economy.

Unemployment measures indicate the extent to which the labor services of a country's people, the single most

---

[3] These and other labor-market statistics are compiled and reported by the Bureau of Labor Statistics online at www.bls.gov.

important resource of an economy, are not fully utilized. As is clear from an inspection of the graph in Figure 10.1, unemployment tends to remain high for several years after a recession (this is especially the case after the most recent ones). Indeed, the unemployment rate only fell below 9 percent a full two years after attaining its peak of 10.1 percent in December 2009. An unemployment rate of this magnitude implies that the economy could produce many more goods and services. For example, the difference between 5 percent – the average of the ten years prior to the recession – and 10 percent represents about 7.5 million people who could have been employed. As the dollar value of goods and services, gross domestic product (GDP), per employed worker in 2010 was $112,000 ($14.6 trillion divided by 130 million workers), a reasonable estimate of the foregone national income during that year is in the order of $840 billion. By comparison, the defense budget for one year is about $700 billion. Of course, the shortfall in GDP is considerably larger, say of the size of the $1.2 trillion deficit of that year, if one also accounts for those working part-time who sought full-time employment. Furthermore, the recession itself was the major factor causing that record deficit, because taxable income falls with unemployment.

The principal reason that unemployment is defined to reflect active job search is that these people are taking part in the job-matching process. The other side of the process is reflected by the number of job openings that employers want to fill. These are measured in the monthly Job Openings and Labor Turnover Survey (JOLTS) conducted by the US census, which asks a sample of employers to report the number of job openings, as well as the number of workers who joined and left employment in the firm during the previous month. Economists have found that the number of searching unemployed workers and the number of job openings are together important determinants of the flow of workers hired in that

Figure 4.3 Job openings and employment

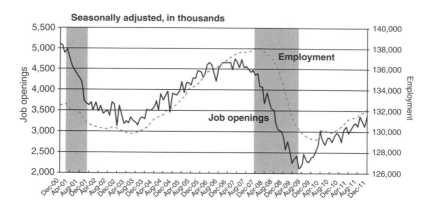

Note: Shaded areas represent recessions as determined by the National Bureau of Economic Research (NBER)
Source: Bureau of Labor Statistics, Current Employment Survey and Job Openings and Labor Turnover Survey, February 7, 2012

month.[4] Indeed, the log of the ratio of the monthly flow of hires from unemployment to the number of unemployed workers, which can be interpreted as probability with which the typical worker finds a job in a certain month, is roughly proportional to the log of the ratio of the number of job openings to the number of actively searching workers. This relationship, derived from that known as the 'matching function', is crucial to understanding the dynamics of the level of unemployment, as is clearly illustrated in Figure 10.3.

The two curves in Figure 4.3 represent the numbers of job openings available in each month, measured on the left vertical axis in thousands of vacancies, and the total employment in the

---

[4] This discovery, along with the model development required to apply it, was cited by the Nobel Committee in awarding the Nobel Prize in Economic Sciences to Peter Diamond, Christopher Pissarides, and myself in 2010.

USA, which corresponds to the measure along the vertical axis on the right of the figure calibrated in thousands of workers. For each month during the last decade, vacancies have fluctuated between 3 and 5 million job openings per month, while total employment varied from a high of 138 million workers in December 2007 at the beginning of the Great Recession to a low of 129 million in December 2009. The shaded areas represent the two most recent recession periods, the first the recession of 2001 and the second the Great Recession of 2009. As is clear, the level of employment follows the movements in the number of job openings with a delay or lag of a few months, as is predicted by the proportional relationship between the log of the hires to unemployment ratio and the log of the ratio of measured job openings to measured unemployment, and the fact that the level of employment changes to balance the difference between the flow of workers hired and the flow who separate from employment in every month.

The fact that it is movements in job openings that generates fluctuations in the level of employment is an important observation. It is the demand for labor, derived from a need for workers to supply goods and services to the economy as a whole, that is the primary driving force behind employment fluctuations. The source of those fluctuations in job openings over the period from August 2003 (the low point of the previous recession) to August 2006 (the date at which openings began to recover after the 2001 recession) is relatively easy to understand. It is also closely related to the causes and consequence of the financial crisis of 2007–8.

The period in which job openings rose sharply, from August 2003 to mid-2006, corresponds closely to the run-up in the prices of residential housing and other real estate at a rate that far exceeded the general rate of inflation in prices of goods and services generally. There were two important responses to this rise in the relative price of real estate. First, homeowning households regarded the increased value of their homes as a form of wealth accumulation. As real estate is the predominant asset in the portfolios of almost all households, households responded to this perceived windfall largely by buying more goods and services, particularly durable goods such as cars, recreation vehicles, pleasure boats, etc. They did so even though the disposable income of the median household had increased only modestly during the period. To finance this surge in expenditure, households added to their debt, in part by borrowing against the increased value of their homes, which banks were willing and able to supply at relatively low interest rates as a consequence of accommodating monetary policy. At the same time, the construction sector cashed in on the increase in prices of their product and the ready availability of credit at low interest rates in order to expand the employment of construction workers and supply more housing units. Next, the boom in employment generated by this surge in the demand for goods and services fed on itself to create more employment in other sectors of the economy.

Asset price bubbles burst, as they must, and when that happens there are dire consequences. In spite of an apparent belief that housing prices never fall – except for a small drop in 1989–90, they had not since the Great Depression – a decline began in 2006. Households had already reduced their expenditures on durable goods, in part because they had recently purchased new items and in part because of the growing need to pay the interest and principal on the newly acquired debt. Furthermore, as the value of their homes fell, they could no longer expand their borrowing and indeed realized that a readjustment of their portfolios to one that included less debt was both desirable and necessary. At the same time, the value of the mortgages held by banks fell, along with the fall of the value of the assets that secured them. A rise in the rate of defaults on these loans further reduced the value of bank capital. The banking crisis was in progress resulting in credit restrictions on employers, particularly those who were starting new businesses, those that disproportionally contribute to the flow of new hires. As a consequence of this combination of falling demand for goods and services, and the credit restrictions that accompany a major banking crisis, the number of job openings tanked – and with it the level of employment.

Government officials and policy makers responded to the crisis with force. The actions taken to stabilize the banking system have already been mentioned. Although the bail-out was very unpopular with the general public – for good reason, as it appeared to benefit those who were responsible for the crisis in the first place – a large majority of economists agree that this action, together with subsequent monetary policy designed to keep banks liquid, prevented a second full-fledged depression in less than 100 years. However, maintaining the existence of the necessary superstructure needed to allocate capital in the economy did not correct the cause of unemployment, the drop in the demand for currently supplied goods and services by households, and the dreary prospects for demand in the near future. This drop in demand reflected the fact that US households – the most economically important group of consumers in the world – wanted to save money in order to reduce their debts. Indeed, many were and are still in danger of losing their homes because they cannot service their mortgages; those who can pay their mortgages find that this is the most important priority in their household budget.

The market response to an excess supply of goods and services, which excessive unemployment represents, should result in two forms of price adjustment that tend to offset the imbalance. First, interest rates should fall, which would encourage households to substitute current for future goods and services. However, the banks were already experiencing high default rates on existing loans and were not about to take on the additional risk. They either refused to lend at all to finance household purchases and business investment, or required higher rates of interest to compensate for the perceived additional risk. The Federal Reserve under the leadership of its chairman Ben Bernanke attempted to offset this effect by pursuing traditional monetary policy designed to lower the rates at which banks pay for funds: the interest rates paid on demand and savings deposits and interbank loans. It became apparent that these actions could not stem the tide, in part because these rates had fallen close to their zero bounds. If negative rates of interest were required to return the economy back to normal, providing them was beyond the ability of traditional monetary policy as we know it. For this reason, the Federal Reserve began an asset-buying strategy designed to affect rates on bonds and other credit instruments of longer maturity, a policy that became known as quantitative easing (QE). Although these actions helped, they did not directly address the principal problem – the shortfall in demand for goods and services relative to the ability of the economy to produce.

As the excess supply for goods and services is directly reflected in an excess supply of labor services, theoretically wage rates should also fall relative to the prices of goods and services, restoring employer incentives to hire workers. In fact, real wage rates did fall relative to trend but so did prices, in part because firms found ways to substantially increase labor productivity. As employers saw no early revival of demand for goods and services, the increases in productivity did not encourage them to expand employment. Instead, it allowed them to improve profit positions further by either laying off more workers or by cheaper part-time workers. For both reasons – falling wages and reduced unemployment – the labor income of households fell quite dramatically. This fall had a further negative effect on household demand for goods and services. Of course, the federal government can offset the reduction in private demand for goods and services by increasing federal expenditures on collective needs – those related to defense, education, and infrastructure. Indeed, President

Obama asked for and received a $787 billion fiscal stimulus package in February 2009, known as the American Recovery and Reinvestment Act, which included a combination of additional federal spending as well as substantial tax cuts for individuals and businesses. In addition to a tax rebate, taxes on payrolls were reduced in order to discourage further layoffs, and the unemployment benefit period was extended to provide disposable income to families experiencing long unemployment spells. There has been considerable controversy over the effect of the spending component of the package. It has been criticized by some for being wasteful and misdirected, and by others for being insufficient in size. In retrospect, responsible professional assessments seem to agree that job losses would have been much larger in 2009 and 2010 without it. Indeed, once the money ran out in 2011, job losses in that year included large numbers of teachers, police, and other public service personnel employed by state and local governments, whose earnings had been financed by the act. Finally, any move to sustain the fiscal stimulus died when the president's party lost control of Congress in November 2010. Instead, the focus was redirected toward the future problems associated with the increase in federal debt that had been accumulated – in no small measure – because of the reduction in tax revenue attributable to the recession.

In the two years since the end of the Great Recession, some economists have pointed to problems other than the lack of aggregate demand for the slow recovery. As evidence, the fact that unemployment did not fall initially in response to the weak recovery in job openings in the first half of 2010 has been used to argue that there are new problems of matching workers to jobs not present before the recession. For example, the well-known academic economist Narayana Kocherlakota, who is also currently president of the Minneapolis Federal Reserve Bank, made the following comment on this fact in an August 2010 speech delivered in Marquette, Michigan: 'What does this change in the relationship between job openings and unemployment connote? In a word, mismatch. Firms have jobs, but can't find appropriate workers ... the Fed does not have the means of transforming construction workers into manufacturing workers.'

That the construction industry was devastated by the collapse in demand for new housing units is beyond question, but the decline in employment in this field is far less than the shortfall in the total. Others have suggested that the inability of households to move to areas where jobs are more plentiful – because their mortgage exceeds the value of their home or a buyer cannot be found – has hampered an important labor-market adjustment mechanism. The extension of unemployment benefits is suggested as another cause of the slow decline in the unemployment rate. However, recent attempts to quantify the effects of these possible causes of unemployment conclude that they are responsible for at most 0.5–1.5 percentage points of the five percentage-point increase in unemployment.[5] That is, were aggregate demand to return to pre-recession levels, then the unemployment rate should fall back to the long-run average of around 6 percent rather than 5 percent.

The year 2011 was one of weak recovery in the private sector, while the public sector contracted dramatically. Indeed, overall gains in employment were not sufficient to offset growth in working-age population until the last few months of the year.

---

[5] Recent studies of the issues include Gadi Barlevy (2011), 'Evaluating the Role of Mismatch for Rising Unemployment', Federal Reserve Bank of Chicago; Aysegul Sahin, Joseph Song, Giorgio Topa, and Giovanni L. Violante (2011), 'Measuring Mismatch in the US Labor Market', Federal Reserve Bank of New York; and Mary Daly, Bart Hobijn, and Robert Valletta (2011), 'The Recent Evolution of the Natural Rate of Unemployment', Federal Reserve Bank of San Francisco.

In the new year of 2012, there were a few signs of renewal in the form of job growth, even in auto and other manufacturing industries. Still prospects for robust growth in the near future are threatened by a new financial crisis and a return to recession in Europe. Higher energy prices induced by unrest in the Middle East also represent a threat to recovery. Hence, the re-employment of the roughly 7 million people needed to return to trend will take far longer than in past recessions. Furthermore, that process is complicated by the fact that many of these people have lost their contact with the world of work, while a large body of new entrants have not had the opportunity to participate in it at all. As a consequence, skills important for future productivity have been lost by the long-term unemployed and not acquired by the young among the unemployed. This additional effect of the Great Recession will add to the unemployment problems of the future.

Obviously, this prognosis is far from the 'good news' that we would like to hear. However, experience suggests that recovery will occur and indeed a new boom based on an exciting new technology that we cannot now foresee may well be in our future. To prepare for that event, we need to collectively invest in the education and innovation that will be needed to produce that future boom, and at the same time to resolve the long-term effects of the financial crisis of 2009, including the additional government debt that it produced.

Chapter 5
A. Michael Spence

BIOGRAPHY

A. MICHAEL SPENCE, USA

ECONOMICS, 2001

In any market or deal there is likely to be one party with an advantage – a seller with a monopoly, a buyer with choices, or any party with greater information that they can use to their benefit. A. Michael Spence, George Akerlof, and Joseph Stiglitz shared the 2001 Nobel Prize in Economics for their analyses of markets with this 'asymmetric' information, which formed the core of modern information economics.

While any individual would like to be in an advantageous position, such imbalances are not always good for the market as a whole. Akerlof, for example, examined how they can cause high interest rates in Third World markets and discrimination in the labor market.

Spence considered ways to improve the balance and identified 'signaling' as a broad brushstroke solution for the market which can also have benefits at an individual level. The idea is simple – better informed parties in a market invest in uniform ways to advertise their benefit to potential partners. Such signals may be costly, and not intrinsically valuable, but raise the level of the market to a generally higher standard and allow it to flow more freely as the 'buyer' has more confidence.

The example Spence gave was education. In an open job market prospective employers need to find the best candidates. By investing in education, society as a whole can benefit by offering a better-qualified workforce, signaling their standard of education on a CV.

Individuals undertaking further education can reap greater benefits even if their education is not intrinsically valuable. A degree in geology, for example, may not be of much use for a job in a theater, but having a degree in itself is a benchmark of intellect, and a good work ethic.

Andrew Michael Spence was born in Montclair, New Jersey, in 1943 to Canadian parents. His father was a member of the War Time Prices and Trades Board, a job which entailed frequent trips to Washington.

He was raised in Canada, where he received an 'excellent and liberating' education at University of Toronto Schools. In 1962 he entered Princeton to study philosophy, and in 1966 won a Rhodes Scholarship to study mathematics at Magdalen College, Oxford. Combining these disciplines, Spence returned to the USA in 1968 to study economics at Harvard, gaining his PhD for his thesis on market signaling in 1972 which, he jokes, 'seemed quite well received' – it won the David A. Wells Prize.

By this time Spence had already been teaching for a year at the Kennedy School of Government at Harvard. He then served a year as associate professor of economics at Stanford – teaching Bill Gates and Steve Ballmer among others – before returning to Harvard as a full professor.

In 1983 Spence became Chairman of the Economics Department and the following year Dean of the Faculty of Arts and Sciences. He stepped down in 1990 to become Dean of the Graduate School of Business at Stanford University, California, until 1999, when he took posts with Oak Hill Capital Partners, the Polaroid Corporation and Siebel Systems.

In 1982 he received the John Bates Clark medal from the American Economic Association. Spence is currently the chairman of an independent Commission on Growth and Development, aimed at encouraging and sustaining high growth in developing countries.

He is a senior fellow at Stanford's Hoover Institution and in 2010 joined the faculty of the Stern School of Business in New York. Spence is married and has three children.

✷　✷　✷　✷　✷

Long-Term Trends and Structural Changes in the Global Economy

INTRODUCTION

The megatrend in the global economy, at least the one that gets my attention, is the growing size and impact of the developing countries. As I argued in *The Next Convergence* (2011), we are just past the midpoint of a century-long journey that began after World War II. At the starting point, say 1950, about 15 percent of the world's population lived in what we now call advanced countries. These are roughly the members of the Organisation for Economic Co-operation and Development (OECD) minus a few recent arrivals. They have incomes in today's US dollars above $20,000 per person per year. They are rich. They have lots of troubles now – and I will come back to that.

The other roughly 85 percent of the world's population had not experienced growth in the previous 200 years. They were not participants in the Industrial Revolution that began in Britain. They were poor. Their incomes varied according to their continent. In south and east Asia, and in Africa, probably US $400 per person per year would be a reasonable average income. Latin America was slightly ahead of that, mainly because Argentina had experienced a period of rapid growth in the first half of the 20th century.

Many thought that this configuration was a permanent state of affairs. But they were wrong. The developing countries began to grow: first a few, then a few more and, in the last 30 years, China and India entered high-growth mode.

Prior to 1750 and the British Industrial Revolution, worldwide growth rates were negligible. Europe and America grew in the following 200 years at around 2 percent in real terms (that is with inflation subtracted out). High growth in the developing countries can be at 7 percent or higher and can be maintained for a long period of time. Why the huge difference? And is there something wrong with the advanced countries that still grow at 2.5 percent when not in a crisis?

Well, the answer is something like this. Professor Robert Solow taught us that long-term growth is caused by technological progress, which causes productivity to rise. In the advanced countries we invent and share that technology. But the developing countries got so far behind that they do not need to invent for quite some time: they can import the technology, or borrow it from us. And that process is a lot faster than inventing the technology. That, basically, is the key to the post-war high growth in developing countries. There is a lot more to it, but that is the core. Of course, during this process, incomes and productivity rise in the developing countries, and thus they become advanced countries. There is nothing more to 'borrow' so they become producers and consumers of technology, like the rest of us. And growth slows down to say 2.5 percent.

Accordingly, for much of the last 60 years we have seen an expanding pattern of growth in developing countries. But these countries began so small and so poor that their growth did not really matter much to us. Advanced countries dominated the global economy in size, power, and governance.

This brings us to what is special about this moment in history. The developing countries are on the verge of becoming more than one-half of the global economy. It is no longer true that they are small, poor, and lacking in impact. China and India are a key part of this. Their populations are 1.3 billion (China) and 1.2 billion (India), and between them they account for almost 40 percent of the population of the planet. They are not rich, yet, and India is behind China, but they are growing. The EU and the USA are the two largest economies in the world, and they are roughly equal in size. China is third and about half the size, but is growing at 8–10 percent and catching up rapidly.

All this means two basic things. One has to do with shares and the other has to do with size. First, let's consider size. If, as seems likely, the major developing countries maintain high growth for the next couple of decades, and then start to slow for the reasons mentioned above, then the global economy will likely triple in size in the next 25 years. This is because growth is deceptive. Twenty-five years ago, China was growing at 10 percent per year and doubling in size every seven years. But it was tiny in absolute terms. Its growth was noteworthy but, at the time, largely irrelevant in terms of impact on the global economy. Now fast forward. China is half the size of the United States. When it grows at 10 percent, the absolute increment to global demand and GDP is huge and is the equivalent of the USA growing at 5 percent, which almost never happens. So you see the point. High growth over decades has made the developing countries large and significant in the global economy, and their future growth will make the global economy huge.

With respect to shares (which always add up to 1 or 100 in percentage terms) the implications are not that complicated. The share of the advanced countries is declining and will continue to decline. The USA, which has been dominating because Europe is not (yet) a unified entity from a governance perspective, will lose its dominance. Notwithstanding the current political dysfunction and gridlock, it is likely to evolve into a highly innovative and successful, medium-sized country, not unlike Germany in terms of share today.

After I had written *The Next Convergence* I was often asked by people in advanced countries: if they (meaning the developing countries) win, do we lose? The short answer is 'yes' in terms of share and influence; but 'no' in terms of economic performance and competitiveness, provided we are on our game. The reason for the latter is that the share growth of the developing countries is accommodated by the growth of the global economy, not by any need for us to shrink.

We could spend time on how developing-economy high growth works, and when it does not work. This is something that I cover in my book, and which is dealt with by the Growth Commission. This is not just a matter of idle curiosity: understanding the economic and political dynamics and the key policies that support this growth helps all kinds of people assess future prospects and related things such as investment opportunities and risks.

Rather than explore that here, instead I focus on the challenges that this rapidly changing structure creates for all of us on the planet. These challenges are huge and will require a generation of sustained effort by today's young, and a good bit of luck as well, to deal with them.

THE NATURAL RESOURCE BASE OF THE ECONOMY

If all this growth occurs using what I will call the old growth model, it probably won't work. Energy supply might last until the end of the 21st century, but it will rise in price. Shale gas, a major potential disruptive technology, might delay that demise. Figure 5.1 shows a picture of the world's projected energy consumption, just to give you an idea.

Other commodities will come into short supply or experience rising relative prices that may cause growth to slow down. Water, which is mispriced almost everywhere, will become a dangerously scarce commodity. The oceans and other habitats are experiencing rapidly diminished stocks and biodiversity, with unknown consequences and potential tipping points.

Then there is climate change, which is too large a subject to go into here. At the moment, the man-made flows of CO_2 in the atmosphere are about 30 billion tons per year. Scientists say that to reduce the probability of fairly extreme upward shifts in average temperatures that figure will have to come

Figure 5.1   Global energy consumption

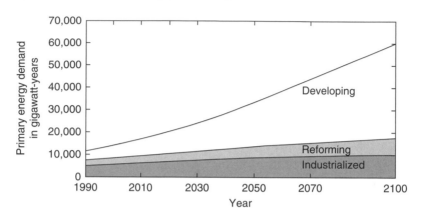

down to closer to 15 billion tons. But a reasonably optimistic forecast of the trajectory we are on with all this growth is that we will get to 60 billion tons per year in about three or four decades. That is an extraordinarily risky path to follow. In this and other dimensions we are playing roulette with the planet, and if we play it for long enough we will lose.

There are two ways to think about this. One, which some in advanced countries subscribe to, is that we have to stop the growth. The argument is that more and more consumption does not make us happier. It may just make us fat. But this will not be acceptable to the developing countries. It is unlikely that it could be imposed as a 'solution' and it would be unfair.

The other option is to invent, over time, a new growth model that is consistent with the natural resource base of the planet. That is the great adventure that we are now on. In important areas like climate change, it requires international cooperation in a complex setting, and thus far, not much concrete evidence of this has emerged. As you can see, I think there are huge distributional issues embedded in finding any solution. They cannot be ignored. The international climate change negotiations focused on long-term, 50-year targets and commitments. As a strategy, this is sure to fail. It is way too risky for any country to agree to long-term targets. No one has any idea how to get there, but we do know how to get started. And there is reason to be optimistic. The energy efficiency of buildings has a huge payoff in itself – and that translates immediately into reduced carbon. As an investment, it pays off over reasonable periods of time. Education about sustainability issues is improving, and values are changing. This will provide a more informed foundation of understanding and support for policies that move economies in the direction of sustainable patterns – in various fields. As I said before, it will take a generation or more of sustained effort. The first part can be done. Then we will need a lot of creativity and a bit of luck in order to get to the endpoint.

EQUITY

There is more to sustainability than natural resources. We face challenges in the areas of stability, equity, and flawed self-limiting growth models that we have to try to deal with too. Let me begin with equity.

Two powerful forces are operating in the global economy. One is technology that automates things and economizes on middle- and lower-skilled labor. The other is the arrival of several hundred million new entrants to increasingly integrated global labor markets, many of those arrivals being initially in the lower-to-middle skill and education range. The result is a very powerful set of forces that have lowered the share of global income going to these groups, and a concomitant rapid rise in the share going to highly educated people and the owners of capital. The result is a very widespread pattern of rising income inequality, with related employment challenges for the lower-to-middle income groups. If I had more space to explore this here, I would take an aside and document this with a rash of data. But that seems a poor use of limited space. It is a fact and it is threatening social cohesion across a broad range of countries and regions, including the Middle East, Western Europe, the United States, China, and others.

These forces that are the underlying cause of the rising income inequalities are not necessarily permanent, but they will not go away quickly either. They are likely to be around for long enough to upset and damage political consensus and policy effectiveness. And it could get worse in terms of violent objections to a system that is perceived to be rigged to favor the rich, the powerful, and the fortunate. Redistributing income, wealth, and opportunity, even over time, will not be easy. But it is crucial.

I put this under the heading of sustainability, because I have come to believe that a breakdown of social cohesion undercuts the effectiveness of political and policy process and governance structures. And I think we know that the latter is the foundation upon which sound economic and social progress is based.

GOVERNANCE

The post-World War II global system was governed largely by the advanced countries. There was the cold war overlay that ended in 1989. And that did distort things, sometimes for the better, often for the worse. Corrupt regimes were supported on both sides, because they supported the 'right' side.

But now we have entered a world in which economic power and influence is distributed over a range of major economies with varying sizes, stages of development, incomes, priorities, and governance structures. If homogeneity is an asset in achieving global coordination, then this is a nightmare. There is an alternative view. It is that a dominant and relatively benign player is an even more stable structure. That may be correct, but we are losing that, and it is not an option going forward. Worse, the advanced countries as a group are experiencing fiscal imbalance, slow growth, and, in Europe's case, negative growth because of imbalances in Europe's structure and high unemployment. So these countries are preoccupied with domestic issues and probably underestimate the extent to which a coordinated international effort would help resolve these problems.

The former global governance system – the place where priorities were set and international coordination of policies was achieved – was the G7, essentially the club of the advanced countries. Its leader was, and still is, the USA. But the G7 is no longer sufficient. To be effective, we need the active involvement of the major developing countries, members of a larger group called the G20. The G20 got something done in the midst of the crisis of 2008, but has not yet managed to be a very effective successor to the G7.

You might ask why this matters. There are two ways to answer that. One is that the alternative is a non-cooperative (Nash) equilibrium – a situation in which everyone is optimizing given what others are doing. Sometimes the non-cooperative equilibrium is fine (that is Pareto optimal – no one can be made better off without making someone worse off), but in governance this is not always so. In multiple areas, such as security, energy, financial regulation and stability, the international monetary system, global climate change, trade and financial openness, the Nash equilibrium is Pareto sub-optimal in a very major way. That means that by cooperating you can achieve better outcomes for everyone than are achieved in the non-cooperative approach.

You will hear this described as the need to provide global public goods. This is the second style of answer. It is the same idea. For example, the US dollar has served as the global currency for several decades. And it still is. Some describe it as the least dirty shirt in the closet. It is tarnished by fiscal stress, high government and current account deficits, and political battles that in the summer of 2012 produced the threat of a technical default caused by an unwillingness of Congress to raise the debt ceiling. That, in combination with rising debt and deficit levels, led to a downgrade of the bond-rating of the US sovereign debt.

So managing the global economy and financial system for openness, stability, fairness, and structural soundness does matter, and that requires cooperation in overseeing and managing the global economy. Without that, it is a somewhat dangerous and volatile place. It means building the competence, authority, and trust of existing or new multinational institutions and, as a corollary, it probably means the delegation of some national sovereignty to supra-national entities. Purely voluntary systems in the day-to-day sense do not seem to work very well, much as systems where paying your taxes is voluntary do not work either.

China, India, Brazil, and others are key to this, China especially so. But China has systemic importance at $6000 of per capita income because of its huge population and potential future size. Within China there is a tension: one group says it is too early for China to shoulder global responsibilities. Another group, and outsiders, say – I believe correctly – that it is not in China's interest to ignore its growing impact. Thus far, the latter are winning the tug of war. But it takes time. And there is no historical precedent for having to take on international governance responsibilities at that relatively early stage of growth and development.

Another barrier is trust and governance. While the trend is toward democratic structures – and that is likely to come in China, too – right now not all these countries are democratic. That makes it harder to form functioning governing groups.

STRUCTURAL CHALLENGES IN THE ADVANCED COUNTRIES

The technological and global forces that I described in the section on equity have created structural adjustment challenges for the advanced economies that are relatively new and difficult. We are only now beginning to acknowledge them and to try to deal effectively with them. It is worth noting that surveys such as the Pew survey of attitudes toward globalization reveal a growing distrust and negative attitude toward globalization, especially in the advanced countries.

There are reasons for this. Figure 5.2 shows a picture of employment creation in the period 1990–2008 in the USA. The tradable side of the economy is the collection of goods and services that can be traded – that is, they can be produced in one country and consumed in another. This is about one-third of the economy. The non-tradable side (things such as government, health care (most of it), construction, retail, restaurants, hotels, etc.) has to be produced domestically. People tend to think that goods trade, and some services now too, and the rest is non-tradable. But this is not really correct. More than one-half of the tradable side in the US is services – such as finance, designing computers, consulting, managing multinational enterprises, and a whole range of business services.

Virtually all the net employment creation was in the non-tradable side. If you then dig a bit deeper and ask, industry or sector by sector, where employment went up and down, you

Figure 5.2 Employment creation in the USA, 1990–2008

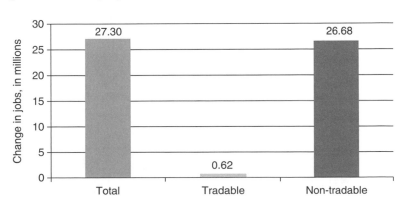

get the following picture as shown in Figure 5.3 (light gray is tradable, dark gray is non-tradable).

If you study this for a while, you will discover that the large employment gains were in government and health care, with significant contributions from construction, until the downturn, and the labor-intensive sectors such as retail and hospitality. On the tradable side, some services in which the USA is competitive grew. The manufacturing sectors declined in employment. When you net out the gains and losses, you get almost no growth in employment in the tradable side.

What is interesting is that manufacturing sectors did not decline in value-added output. That means that value added

Figure 5.3 Employment gains and losses by sector in the US economy

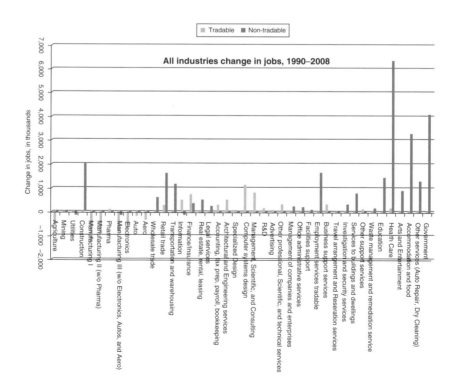

per person employed rose quickly. And it strongly suggests that what happened is that a combination of labor-saving technology and global outsourcing removed the lower-value-added, less skilled jobs from these and to some extent other sectors.

These data do not tell you what to conclude, but they do strongly suggest that the US economy prior to the crisis was on an unsustainable growth path with excess consumption (both private and government) enabled by leverage or debt, and with a boost from asset bubbles. Investment on the public sector side was deficient, and that probably caused private sector domestic investment to be too low, too. The crisis caused this growth pattern to break down, and we are in the midst of a difficult transition to a different and more sustainable growth pattern. It will be painful. It will also be slow because it is very hard for the political process to settle the issue of burden sharing in the transition. And thus far it is unclear whether the challenge is well understood. I guess I would say that there has been slow progress on problem recognition. There is a tendency to regard the crisis as a hundred-year storm, rather than a recipe that was not going to turn out very well after being in the oven for a long time. There is much more to be said about this, but I do not have space here.

CONCLUSIONS

The post-war period saw the developing countries experience real growth for the first time. Hundreds of millions of people have escaped poverty, with more to do so. Incomes and opportunities are rising. In human terms, it is truly a stupendously positive set of trends and, by and large, the future looks bright. It will probably continue, though there will be bumps along the way.

But all this growth has brought us to the point where there are new global challenges and there are new and slightly bewildering problems in advanced countries, ones for which old mindsets are poorly matched. These challenges include rising inequality and the potential for political and social turmoil, significant issues of stability, both medium- and long-term sustainability issues having to do with natural resources, and also unbalanced and self-limiting growth models.

There is a large agenda before us, with contributions needed from a wide range of sub-disciplines in economics and political economy. For young researchers it might be called a target-rich environment. It is an interesting one, and a risky one as well.

REFERENCES

El-Erian, Mohamed, and Spence, Michael. 2012. Multiple equilibria, systemic risk and market dynamics: what you need to know and why. *Financial Analyst Journal*, 68(5). http://www.pimco.com/ EN/Insights/Pages/Systemic-Risk,-Multiple-Equilibria-and-Market-Dynamics-What-You-Need-to-Know-and-Why-.aspx.

Spence, Michael. 2011. *The Next Convergence: The Future of Economic Growth in a Multispeed World*. New York: Farrar, Straus, and Giroux.

Spence, Michael. 2011. Globalization and unemployment: the downside of integrating markets. *Foreign Affairs*, July/August.

Spence, Michael, and Hlatshayo, Sandile. 2011. The evolving structure of the American economy and the employment challenge. Working paper, Council on Foreign Relations.

The Growth Report: Strategies for Sustained Growth and Inclusive Development. A report by the Commission on Growth and Development. World Bank. http://web.worldbank.org/WBSITE/ EXTERNAL/EXTABOUTUS/ORGANIZATION/EXTPREMN ET/0,,contentMDK:23225680~pagePK:64159605~piPK:6415766 7~theSitePK:489961,00.html.

Chapter 6
Finn E. Kydland

BIOGRAPHY

FINN E. KYDLAND, NORWAY/USA

ECONOMICS, 2004

*Macroeconomics is a delicate balancing act for government
policymakers, whose aim is to keep inflation low and to foster*

an environment to boost manufacturing and employment, thus creating long-term growth. But time is not on their side. Inconsistencies creep in, which can ultimately result in policies leading to high inflation – the opposite of their stated aim.

One factor in tripping up policies is fluctuation in business cycles. Traditionally this had been put down simply to variations in consumer demand, but in two joint papers, in 1977 and 1982, Kydland and fellow Laureate Edward Prescott offered new approaches to the subject. It was their 1977 paper, 'Rules rather than discretion: the inconsistency of optimal plans', that highlighted the problems of time consistency for policymakers. They went on to analyze the driving forces behind business cycles in their 1982 paper 'Time to build and aggregate fluctuations'. Their work gave a new insight into the subject and laid the foundations for the 'new-Keynesian' approach to business cycles, and was recognized by the Nobel Committee in awarding them the Prize in Economics in 2004.

Finn Erling Kydland was born in 1943 on his grandparents' farm in Bjerkreim, Norway, and grew up in rural Soyland, about 25 miles south of Stavanger. He was the eldest of six children and the only child in his class to progress beyond a very basic elementary education, going at 15 to high school in Bryne. He credits his education there – particularly in mathematics – with giving him the choice of Norway's universities, but while pondering his decision he took a teaching post at Oltedal elementary school. There a colleague employed him as his accountant and business partner, sparking an interest in business and economics.

As a result, Kydland applied to the Norwegian School of Economics (NHH), which initially rejected him, but after he completed a business correspondence course while performing National Service, in 1965 he was admitted.

After receiving his BSc in 1968, Kydland became a research assistant to his professor, Sten Thore. Kydland followed Thore to Carnegie Mellon University in Pittsburgh in 1969.

Among his tutors were Robert Lucas, whom Kydland recalls working through his own Nobel-winning theory over the course of a few lectures; David Cass, who first encouraged Kydland to expand an idea about non-cooperative and dynamic games into a thesis; and Robert Kaplan, his main advisor. When the proposed thesis was accepted, however, it was another new tutor, and future long-term writing partner, Edward Prescott, who became Kydland's mentor for his PhD dissertation 'Decentralized Macroeconomic Planning'.

After earning his PhD in 1973, Kydland returned to Norway to teach at the NHH. Prescott joined him the following year as visiting professor. In 1976 Kydland returned to the US as visiting professor at the University of Minnesota, followed by an appointment as associate professor at Carnegie Mellon.

He remained there until 2004, before joining the University of California at Santa Barbara where he is the Henley Professor of Economics. At UCSB he founded the Laboratory for Aggregate Economics and Finance. He holds the Richard P. Simmons Distinguished Professorship at the Tepper School of Business at Carnegie Mellon, and a part-time position as Adjunct Professor at the NHH. He is a Research Associate for the Federal Reserve Banks of Dallas and St Louis, and a Senior Research Fellow at the IC2 Institute at the University of Texas at Austin.

Kydland is married and has four children and two step-children.

✳   ✳   ✳   ✳   ✳

On Policy Consistency

To what extent does government economic policy affect incentives in the decision-making of people and businesses, preferably in a good way from the point of view of society, but perhaps at times in a bad way? In light of what has happened in the past few years in economies all over the world, this is an especially timely question.

The field of macroeconomics deals with entire nations, or the interaction among multiple nations. While macroeconomics is concerned with the aggregate (that is, the sum across all relevant units) of the consumption decisions of millions of individuals and households, for example, and the investment decisions (building factories, purchasing machines, erecting office buildings) of thousands of businesses, it is important to consider the incentives of all the individual decision makers who make those decisions.

An example may be instructive at this point. Suppose a firm contemplates investing in a factory, costing perhaps tens or hundreds of millions of dollars. This is a large expense to incur in the course of the construction period, during which the factory will produce nothing to be sold. Presumably, in order to have the incentive to go ahead with this project, the firm would be quite confident that it can more than make up for the cost in the form of income over the factory's life, perhaps ten or twenty years, from selling the products for which it was designed.

This factory, when completed, becomes part of the nation's stock of productive capital. The nation's capital is combined with labor input – that is, workers of various skills – to produce output of goods and services (some consumed by households, some used by businesses as investment in new capital, some used by federal and state and local governments), what in the statistics is called real gross domestic product (GDP). The total income from doing so can be divided into labor income, going to the workers in the forms of wages and salaries, and capital income, compensating the business owners.

ROLE OF GOVERNMENT

In order for governments to provide the services they do, they need to generate enough revenue to cover their costs. Two major sources of revenues are taxes on capital and labor income. If the business owner knows that out of every dollar earned he has to pay the government 30 cents, then that would be taken into account in the estimate of whether or not building the factory will eventually pay off. Interestingly, suppose that after a couple of years of operation of the factory the government were to pull a surprise by announcing that, from now on, one instead has to pay 40 cents in taxes out of every dollar of income. That could easily turn a project (here, the building of the new factory) from being profitable to one that the owners, after the fact, wish they had passed on. But now, of course, as the cost has already been incurred, most likely it would not be in the firm's interest to shut down the factory.

Another way in which the government can affect the future profitability of a factory is by imposing new regulatory constraints that make it costlier to operate. In some countries, it may even be rational to worry about whether the factory, at some point in the future, might be confiscated (nationalized) by the government, with little or no compensation.

EXPECTATIONS OF FUTURE POLICY

The main point is that the business owner's impression of what the policy environment will be like for many years into the future plays an important role for the decision to invest today. Moreover, the government has the potential to inject considerable uncertainty into the calculations needed to decide whether such new investment projects will be profitable or not.

One can come up with many such examples of the importance of expectations about future government behavior for decisions made today by individuals and businesses. A potentially dramatic one relates to the government debt. I mentioned above that capital and labor income taxation are important sources of revenues for the government. So are sales taxes, property taxes, duties, and other sources. But what if these revenues, in a given year, say, do not cover the desired amount of government expenditures? Then the government may borrow the difference (if it can). That is, the government debt increases. At times, and in some countries, this increase in government debt would reach unsustainable levels. So rather than repay the debt, as one would expect responsible governments to do, in the history of many nations one has seen them essentially reneging on most or all of their current debt. That is to say, typically they don't renege officially. Instead they do so indirectly by speeding up the money printing presses, sometimes even to the extent of creating what we call a hyperinflation, during which prices over some period rise at annual rates into the hundreds or thousands of percent.

It is easy to find such examples, from the post-World War I hyperinflation in Germany after the nation was saddled with war reparations and therefore a huge increase in its debt, to the modern case of Zimbabwe. I have in my possession an official banknote issued in 2008 by the Federal Bank of Zimbabwe on which it says 50 trillion dollars. I presume, at the time, one could purchase virtually nothing for this piece of cash, as prices continued to surge ahead. For a while around the 1980s, several Latin American nations, such as Argentina and

Bolivia, engineered spectacular hyperinflations. The economist Philip Cagan, in 1956, wrote an article that included a survey of the hyperinflations up until his time of writing. The record was held by Hungary in the mid-1940s. Typically, prices will increase the fastest right before the hyperinflation finally comes to an end. Cagan's table of hyperinflations indicates that, for Hungary, in the month of the greatest price increase, prices on the average tripled every day. To get a sense of what that means, suppose a hamburger, say, cost $1 on the first day of the month, $3 on the second, $9 on the third, $27 on the fourth, and so on. You can readily calculate that, by the middle of the month (even if it were February), the price of a hamburger would exceed one million dollars!

One can also imagine someone, at the beginning of the month, being in possession of a government bond (non-indexed, to be precise) for the amount of $1000. After only a few days, the bond would be worth virtually nothing in terms of what it could purchase. This illustrates a way in which a government can pretty much rid itself of loads of debt, of course in the process inflicting pain on large numbers of its population: for example, pensioners who would see their savings – intended to get them through their retirement age – evaporate virtually in front of their eyes.

INCOME INEQUALITY ACROSS THE GLOBE

The disparity in nations' income levels, say as measured by income per capita according to official statistics, is tremendous. To be sure, measured income may provide a skewed picture of the associated welfare of the typical citizen of that nation. In some countries, an extensive informal sector (black markets) means that many people are better off than the statistics suggest. In other cases, the statistics on per-capita income may mask considerable inequality within that nation. Still, we have to take the statistics seriously, especially when the differences are large. Western European nations, along with countries such as the United States, Canada, Australia, Japan, Korea, and Taiwan have annual per-capita incomes of about $30,000 and higher. Lots of nations hover in the $10,000–20,000 range. And then we have all those poor nations, many in Africa, with per-capita incomes under $5000, some even under $1000. Zimbabwe is officially listed as having a yearly per-capita income under $100!

Figures 6.1 and 6.2 display these contrasts. Figure 6.1 pictures per-capita real GDP in a diverse set of nations (all the numbers are in constant 2005 dollars; that is, they are inflation adjusted. To convert to 2013 dollars, one needs to raise them all by about 17 percent). Some are notable for rather healthy and steady growth rates, trying to catch up with the United States and Canada. These include Korea, Taiwan, Hong Kong, and Japan, although Japan has faltered somewhat in the

Figure 6.1   Real GDP for several countries

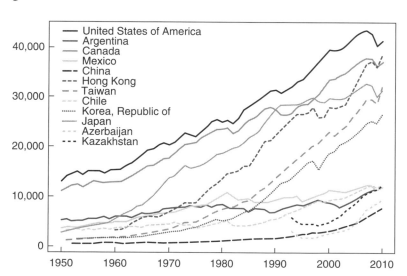

Source: Penn World Table 7.1 (base year = 2005)

Figure 6.2   Real GDP for African nations

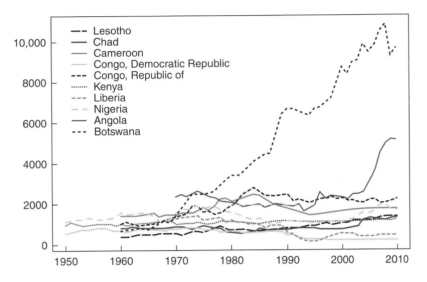

Source: Penn World Table 7.1 (base year = 2005)

past 15–20 years. Some countries were at fairly similar levels around the 1960s, but have since grown much more slowly than those other countries. They include Argentina, Chile, and Mexico. Included are two nations that were created after the break-up of the Soviet Union, namely Azerbaijan and Kazakhstan. These are both resource-rich nations that seem to have put that wealth to reasonably good use (note that a given steepness of a curve near the bottom of the chart corresponds to much higher rate of growth than does that same steepness near the top of the chart). Finally, considering the attention China gets for its size, it may surprise you to see its low per-capita GDP.

Figure 6.2 depicts a set of African nations. Observe the different scale on the vertical axis as compared with Figure 6.1. If I hadn't included Botswana, another relatively resource-rich nation, I could have got by with a scale going to about $5000, as opposed to about $40,000 in Figure 6.1.

TIME INCONSISTENCY OF OPTIMAL POLICY

What can account for such immense disparities? The evidence suggests that in large part it comes down to the nature of nations' governments, political systems and institutions, the presence of corruption or lack thereof, and so on. But, perhaps surprisingly, there is a potential source of problems even for the more well-to-do nations. One may refer to it as *The Time Inconsistency of Optimal Government Policy*. That's a mouthful, and I'll try to give a sense of what it means (see also Kydland and Prescott 1977).

For now, let's imagine an 'ideal' world. Suppose there were a way to quantify, using a mathematical formulation, the welfare of the nation's citizens, today and into the future. A benign policy maker could then select policy (including tax policy) for the indefinite future so as to maximize the expression for the citizens' welfare. We may call that *optimal policy*. Naturally, this policy would take into account the effect that the portion of it pertaining to the future has on earlier decisions, such as the effect that future capital-income taxes have in the investment example above. In general, such a policy would represent a prescription for what to do under various pre-specified circumstances (as governments are not the *only* source of uncertainty in the world!).

As this policy is being implemented, suppose everything is moving along hunky-dory. But suppose also, after five years, say, the policy maker (or some hot-shot quantitative expert in his office) gets the bright idea of recalculating the optimal policy from that point on. That really ought to be unnecessary, since in our ideal world the original calculated plan includes a blueprint for what to do for the upcoming future as well. But suppose one goes ahead anyway. To everyone's surprise, perhaps, a completely different policy path will be found from the continuation of the original plan. The implication seems to be that policy must change, in the interest of the nation's citizens. No! Indeed, theory suggests that if the policy maker falls for the temptation to change, it could be very bad for society.

What is the intuition for this inconsistency over time? Suppose we refer to year 0 as the year in which the original policy plan was determined. As mentioned, this policy took into account, among other things, the effect that policy (for example tax policy) from year 5 and beyond would have on private decisions (such as investment) in years 0, 1, 2, 3, and 4. But when year 5 arrives, those decisions for years 0–4 have already been made. So in the recalculation in year 5, only the policy effects on investment and other private-economy decisions in year 5 and beyond would be taken into account, resulting in a completely different policy prescription than the continuation of the original plan. In particular, it would surely suggest raising taxes on the income from capital that has already been built, with the promise of reducing taxes to previous levels in the future. The government might try to justify the change by arguing that it is facing a near-emergency situation. But potential investors would have to worry about the possibility of the policy maker pulling that one off again in the future. Even the mere uncertainty about whether or not it would happen again could be enough to depress investment activity and therefore longer-term growth of the economy.

Now you may ask (and it is a good question): if this is the situation under 'ideal' circumstances, then what about the more realistic world where policy is chosen under all kinds of political pressure from interest groups and others? Well, that should make it all the more likely that time inconsistency will rear its ugly head, especially in nations with weak institutions and poor property rights. Indeed, once one has understood this problem, an amazing number of developments in nations' economic histories can be seen in a new light.

BENEFITS OF A COMMITMENT MECHANISM

An implication of this theory is that it is advantageous to shield policy making from political pressure, as kind of a commitment mechanism to ensure that promised good policy will be carried out in the future. This principle has been understood and implemented by several nations in the arena of monetary policy, which is carried out by central banks that are independent, to varying degrees, depending on the nation. For example, the Bundesbank in Germany for decades was regarded as the champion of consistency and transparency in their policy making. The Federal Reserve Bank in the United States has not been far behind, in that sense. The Bank of England was formally made independent in 1997. The central banks in Scandinavia are generally regarded to be quite independent.

At the other end of the spectrum are central banks such as that of Argentina. One sign of a central bank's independence is that the president or chairperson remains in that position for a number of years. In the United States, for example, Ben Bernanke is only the sixth chairperson since 1951. Argentina's central bank has had 54 presidents over the 67-year period since 1945 – an average of only 1.25 years per president. In the especially tumultuous two years of 2001–2, the head of the central bank changed four times.

Argentina is an interesting case in that it tried a different commitment mechanism – a currency board. In 1990, the nation was attempting to recover from the awful decade of the 1980s – the so-called lost decade, which ended in hyperinflation, defaults on government debt, losses of pensions, and during which the nation's output per capita had dropped by well over 20 percent. Figure 6.3 shows real GDP per working-age person over much of the post-World War II period. (Note that, unlike Figures 6.1 and 6.2, this chart is on proportional scale. In practice, that is done by plotting the natural logarithm of each of the underlying numbers. In such a plot, a constant growth rate is shown

Figure 6.3   Real GDP per working-age person (log scale) for Argentina

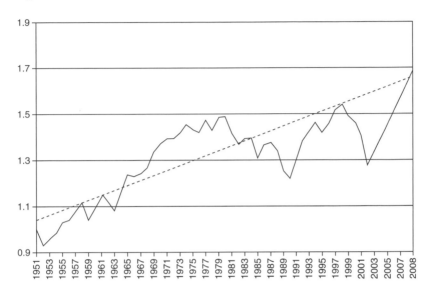

as a straight line, for example the drawn one representing the average growth over the entire period, instead of a steeper and steeper line.) When Carlos Menem became president in 1990 he decided, in order to raise the confidence among investors in his nation, to make the Argentine peso exchangeable one for one with the dollar, accumulating enough dollar reserves to make that policy credible. To the naked eye (as in Figure 6.3), looking at growth rates over the next half-dozen years, this policy seemed to work well. But then, starting around 1998, it all fell apart. Output per capita fell again by over 20 percent, this time over a much shorter period of less than five years; the peso had to be devalued, that is, each dollar suddenly corresponded to multiple pesos; bank deposits were frozen, and all sorts of bad things transpired in the economy.

The explanation usually given for the failure of this 'commitment mechanism' is that, while Argentina seemed to have fixed their monetary problems, they forgot about fiscal policy,

Figure 6.4   Real GDP for Western European nations

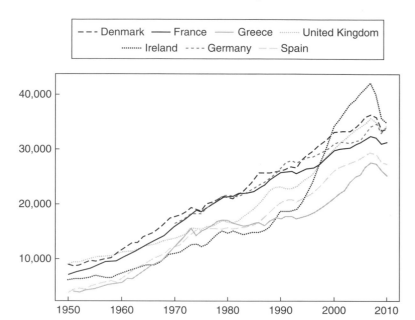

Source: Penn World Table 7.1 (base year = 2005)

that is, tax and spending policy. Monetary policy cannot be completely separate from fiscal policy. For one thing, both are part of the same budget constraint. Yes, the government is subject to a budget constraint just as you and I and everyone else are subject to such constraints. The provinces borrowed heavily, even in the seemingly good times of the 1990s. When it became clear they couldn't meet their debt obligations, they came running to the federal government who had to bail them out, and federal debt ballooned. That is when everything fell apart.

As an indication of how bad things can get when the 'time-inconsistency disease' attacks, consider the behavior of Argentina's stock of business capital per working-age person, which in a healthy nation ought to grow steadily over the long run. Its level peaked in 1982. As of 2008, the last year for which comparable data are available, this ratio was still about 10 percent below its 1982 level. It's a good bet that, even three decades after 1982, it is still below.

An opposite example is Ireland over that same time period, from 1990 until the early 2000s. Starting in the 1960s and 1970s, Ireland had made secondary education free of charge. As a consequence, by 1990 the nation found itself with a potentially skillful workforce, but not enough factories and machines with which to put all of these skills to use. So the government decided to do their best to remove any uncertainty about future taxation. They announced that if you set up shop in Ireland, whether an Irish citizen or a foreigner, these will be your (not very high) tax rates in 1992, 1993, and so on, all the way to 2009. Of course there may have been other favorable factors as well. The bottom line is that Ireland grew spectacularly (have you heard of the Celtic Tiger?). In the course of about a dozen years it went from being one of the lower per-capita-income countries in Western Europe to one of the highest (see Figure 6.4). But alas, this story does not have a happy ending, on account of policy makers panicking at the onset of the financial crisis in 2008. In the last few years of the economic boom, a debt-driven property boom took hold. When property prices plunged in 2008, major Irish banks faced insolvency. The government made the highly questionable decision to bail them out, in the process saddling tax payers with a huge increase in government debt. This ending, however, does not take away from the lesson of the experience in the 1990s, when removal of uncertainty about the tax environment for the foreseeable future encouraged many companies, including foreign ones, to establish and expand productive capacity in Ireland.

REBUILD CREDIBILITY?

An interesting question is: if a nation, such as Argentina, falls prey to the 'time inconsistency disease', how easy is it to rebuild its credibility? The answer has to be, not easy at all. As already mentioned, Argentina, after the lost decade of the 1980s, seemed to grow at acceptable rates. It is possible, however, to 'check the temperature' of a nation using a standard economic model as the 'thermometer'. As reported in Kydland and Zarazaga (2007), using the best available measurements of the nation's level of technology, if Argentina were healthy it should have grown substantially faster even over this period. In particular, the capital stock in the data grew much more slowly than the model suggested ought to have been the case. This indicates that, in spite of President Menem's best intentions, the nation still suffered from lack of credibility among potential investors.

BUT THE MERE CONSISTENCY OF POLICY IS NOT SUFFICIENT

It is important to emphasize that policy consistency is not *sufficient* for healthy growth. Notice the word *optimal* in the description on page 86 above of the basic time inconsistency problem. It would not be good if a country carried out a consistent, but *bad*, policy. One may argue that China is such an example. Its economic policy certainly appears quite consistent. Admittedly, China has made important strides toward greater development, although its income per capita is still very low by international standards.

A stylized description of how nations grow in the long run is as follows. Entrepreneurial and innovative activity takes place, resulting in new and better ways of producing things: new production processes, new products, often with the help of considerable research and development. Factories, machines, and office buildings are needed to implement these innovative ideas. Workers are hired. And so on. In order to facilitate all of this activity, a healthy banking system, or financial system, more

generally, is important, as many of these forward-looking decisions cannot be undertaken without the ability to borrow the
necessary funds.

As documented in an article by Song, Storesletten, and
Zilibotti (2011), in China almost all banks are state owned.
These banks favor the state-owned companies. These state-
owned companies have easy access to credit and, so far, at
least, to cheap labor. They do not need to be very innovative
and productive to show profits. In the meantime, the entre-
preneurs with the really innovative new ideas for products
or ways of doing things have a hard time getting the necessary loans. Typically, they have to save up in advance before
they can implement their ideas. Naturally, activities that are
relatively intensive in labor rather than capital are easier to
finance, as the initial set-up costs are smaller. The overall
result is considerable waste of resources. It is a good bet that
unless China opens up for more competition in the financial
sector, this problem will eventually hurt their ability to grow
at acceptable rates in the long run.

SOME FINAL COMMENTS ON RECENT EVENTS

These ideas provide food for thought about what is going on
currently in many areas of the world, including in the United
States and Western Europe. In the United States, real per-
capita GDP declined in 2008 and 2009 to more than 10 percent below the trend that had prevailed from 1947 to 2007,
and it has so far shown no sign of moving back toward that
old trend. Unemployment has remained high for over four
years. Government debt has risen dramatically, in the face of
dire predictions about further increases as the so-called baby
boomers retire, with predictable demands on the expenditure
side of the government budget constraint. Are potential innovators and investors in new productive capacity holding back

because they are worried that the fruits of such activities will be taxed more heavily in the future? Will the United States catch at least a sneeze of time inconsistency?

In Europe, the eurozone, with its fixed exchange rate among a large number of countries, was conceived with seemingly little attention to enforceable fiscal rules to accompany the new monetary arrangement. As we know, some nations borrowed heavily and have had to be bailed out. Even *within* a nation, such as Spain, much unchecked accumulation of debt by the provinces has taken place. One is reminded of Argentina in the 1990s.

It is probably fair to say that an unprecedented amount of uncertainty prevails about future economic policy in European Union countries as well as in the United States. In Europe, we have seen politicians reacting to short-run developments without any clear plan for next year and beyond. As has been argued in this chapter, this kind of uncertainty is likely to be bad for growth over the next few years. One cannot fault potential innovators and investors in business capital if they choose to wait on the sidelines for a while. Worse, the insights from the time inconsistency literature give reasons to be pessimistic as to whether this uncertainty will be removed soon in any meaningful way.

Admittedly, these problems pale in comparison with the situation in large parts of Africa, as illustrated in Figure 6.2. One of the most pressing and challenging issues in economics is to figure out how nations that are poor can begin to catch up in a significant way.

REFERENCES

Cagan, Phillip. 1956. The monetary dynamics of hyperinflation. In *Studies in the Quantity Theory of Money*, ed. M. Friedman. Chicago: University of Chicago Press.

Heston, Alan, Summers, Robert, and Aten, Bettina. 2012. Penn world table version 7.1. *Center for International Comparisons of Production, Income and Prices.* University of Pennsylvania.

Kydland, Finn E., and Prescott, Edward C. 1977. Rules rather than discretion: the inconsistency of optimal plans. *Journal of Political Economy* 85 (June), 473–491.

Kydland, Finn E., and Zarazaga, Carlos E. J. M. 2007. Argentina's lost decade and the subsequent recovery puzzle. In *Great Depressions of the Twentieth Century,* ed. T. J. Kehoe and E. C. Prescott. Federal Reserve Bank of Minneapolis, 191–216.

Song, Zheng, Storesletten, Kjetil, and Zilibotti, Fabrizio. 2011. Growing like China. *American Economic Review* 101 (February) 196–233.

Chapter 7
Robert M. Solow

BIOGRAPHY

ROBERT M. SOLOW, USA

ECONOMICS, 1987

To keep pace with inflation and rising populations, the economy should ideally be in a constant state of growth. But what is the best way to feed the economy? Robert Solow created a new model, often called the Solow–Swan neoclassical growth model as it was also independently created by Trevor W. Swan, which could separate various factors into inputs (capital and labor) and technology.

By using this model, first published in 1956, Solow calculated that 80 percent of any increase in productivity could be attributed to new technology, the only sustainable source of such growth. But when it came to capital, Solow was a fan of the new. He created a growth model that examined different vintages of capital and concluded that new capital is more valuable, as it is produced through new technology with greater potential for improvement and growth.

Other economists have since adapted or improved Solow's models to produce alternative results, but economists still use his model to estimate the effects of the three main variables: capital, labor and technology. For his ground-breaking work he was awarded the Nobel Prize in Economics in 1987 and the US National Medal of Science in 1999.

He has also contributed to macroeconomic questions of policy and unemployment, as well as the economic management of natural resources.

Robert Merton Solow was born in Brooklyn, New York, in 1924 and was the oldest of three children. He attended local schools where he excelled and in 1940 gained a scholarship to Harvard College, where he studied sociology, anthropology and economics. When America joined World War II Solow interrupted his education to sign up for the army, serving in North Africa and Italy. He returned to Harvard in 1945 and continued to study economics under Wassily Leontief, acquiring an interest in statistics and probability models.

To study statistics more intensively, in 1949 Solow took a fellowship year at Columbia University, while also working on his PhD thesis. Before going to Columbia he was offered the post of assistant professor at Massachusetts Institute of Technology (MIT), where he taught statistics and econometrics from 1950 onward.

By chance, at MIT he was given the office next to that of Paul Samuelson and the pair became good friends and partners in a number of projects, including the von Neumann growth theory (1953), theory of capital (1956), linear programming (1958), and the Phillips curve (1960).

In 1961 Solow won the American Economic Association's John Bates Clark Award, given to the best economist under 40 (he would later be president of the AEA). That same year he was made senior economist for the US government's Council of Economic Advisors and from 1968 to 1970 served as a member of the President's Commission on Income Maintenance. He was a member of the National Science Board from 1995 to 2000.

In 1995 Solow retired from MIT. He has left a strong legacy – several of his students, including Peter Diamond, Joseph Stiglitz, and George Akerlof, have gone on to win the Nobel Prize.

He was also one of the founding directors of the Manpower Demonstration Research Corporation, a research group aimed at improving the employment and earning power of disadvantaged groups. He remains a critic of modern economic approaches to the labor and product markets.

Solow is married and has three children.

Natural Resources and Sustainability

INTRODUCTION

Citizens often have to make up their minds about issues of social and economic policy, with nothing to guide them but vague intuitions and a few stray facts. One function of economic analysis is to help people in this matter. It does this, when it can, by picking out the main factors that influence the outcomes of alternative policy choices, perhaps measuring them and measuring the strength of their influence, and also defining their relation to one another. This last is important because it often turns out that better achievement of one goal necessarily means worse achievement of another. In other words, there are inevitable trade-offs. Economics can sometimes make it clear what the consequences of different policies might be, and why. Careful analysis often shows that what looked at first like matters of 'yes' or 'no' are really matters of 'more or less'. What economic analysis cannot do is to make the citizens' decision for them. That requires more than just analysis.

The examples that I have in mind all have to do with, in one way or another, the interplay between natural resources and the economy. Some natural resources are non-renewable ('exhaustible'). For example, it is a fair approximation that there is only a certain amount of copper in the ground available for human use. Some of it is more cheaply available than the rest, and we do not know with certainty how much there is at what cost; in addition, copper can be partially recycled. These are complications, but the basic problem is the finiteness of the resource base and the fact that what is used now cannot be used later. Some resources, such as forest timber stands and fish populations, are renewable. However, they can be badly used, and destroyed. We have all heard of overfishing and deforestation. But they can also be simultaneously used and preserved, perhaps at a cost. This is a more cheerful situation, but analytically a bit more difficult because of this 'demographic' aspect. The economics of forests and fisheries is an old and well-debated subject, yet it is still important. The natural environment is also a natural resource. It can be 'used', but there is still a choice between damage/destruction and preservation, and environmental economics is in the business of clarifying these choices.

EXHAUSTIBLE RESOURCES

One way to start thinking clearly about non-renewable resources is to invent an artificially simple case. Imagine that there is one cake to be divided between two identical twins. No problem: divide it equally. Now suppose that the (large) cake is to be divided among a hundred people. They are unlikely to be identical siblings, but we can agree that, as citizens, they should be treated equally in this context. Thus the cake should be divided evenly among them. There is an important reason, apart from symmetry, as to why equal division is appropriate. Most of us find it plausible that the first bite of cake is very nice, the second bite is also very pleasant, but a little less so than the first, and the third a little less pleasurable than the second, and so on. This speaks for equal division: if we start with equal division, and then take a little cake from you and give it to me, you will lose a bigger pleasure than I gain. This kind of reasoning has played an important part in economics. (Suppose one of the twins happens to be richer than the other, and already has a lot of cake, what then? The same kind of reasoning leads to a slightly more complicated answer.)

Now suppose the cake (or an oil or copper deposit) has to be divided over time among successive generations. Unless there is a good reason as to why some generations should be favored over others, the principle would seem to be the same. Here a problem arises, however. As the number of generations increases, equal division results in each having a very small share in the initial stock of copper. If we want to plan 'for ever', then the share for each generation dwindles to zero. In fact, the 'for ever' problem has no good solution. Economists have tried to get around this difficulty by 'discounting' future generations, so that very distant generations count for very little. On this complicated calculation, later generations get less than earlier ones, just because they come later. The trouble, however, is that this approach violates our intuition about equal treatment for all. This question of how to deal rationally with the very distant future remains a matter of debate, particularly in dealing with policies toward climate change.

In fact, most natural resources do not enter the economy as direct consumption goods (such as fish, for example) but rather as inputs (such as oil or copper) into the manufacture of consumption goods. This is a big change and leads to more interesting economics. The main difference is that most of the time 'final consumption' goods can be produced using more or less natural resources, and less or more of other things. For example, more precise machining and careful design can reduce the amount of steel or aluminum required to make automobile parts. In that case, the things being substituted for metals are the services of capital equipment and human capital as well as ordinary labor. It may be possible, at least in theory, to produce a constant flow of consumer goods with a steadily dwindling use of non-renewable metals, offset by increasing inputs of capital and labor and renewable resources, all within the limits set by the original stock of scarce natural resources. Technological progress is another important factor, whether in the form of new production processes or of new goods with lower content of scarce natural resources. If there is any practical path to sustainability, it must lie in this direction.

Here another broad question comes to the surface. When we speak of sustainability, what is it that we are trying to sustain or preserve? The idea cannot be to preserve the world exactly as it is. Of course, we would not consider demolishing the Parthenon in order to put up windmills on the Acropolis, or fill in the Grand Canyon to make a field for solar panels. But the Parthenon and the Grand Canyon must be exceptions. If we were forbidden to use up the copper and iron in the earth, or to turn any of the coastline into ports, we would be reduced to a pre-industrial standard of living, and that would be widely unacceptable. It makes more sense to understand that sustainability means preserving for future generations the capacity to enjoy a level of well-being or a standard of living at least as good as our own. In narrowly economic terms, we can translate 'standard of living' into consumer goods and services, though perhaps different ones from those common today. (Even at this narrow level, further complications are possible. Most people care about the well-being of their children and grandchildren. And since they in turn care about their descendants, we have to say that most people care about the distant future. Must we translate that definition into our calculations of sustainability? I suppose in principle, yes, but doing so makes measurement and calculation much more difficult.)

RENEWABLE RESOURCES

Most of these considerations apply also to the case of renewable resources. It is a broad class. One thinks first of living populations that reproduce themselves unless badly disturbed; that is why I have mentioned fish and forests. But agricultural land, or its fertility, is a renewable resource. So are wind and sunlight as sources of energy (at least on any timescale that we can think about). The most interesting question remains: what are the possible patterns of use over time, and what management policies can achieve them? In the non-renewable case, what is used today is simply no longer available for the future (after taking account of recycling). In the case of logging, for instance, the situation is different: if the volume of timber cut this year is no greater than the natural annual growth, the volume of standing timber can be unchanged, or may actually increase, even while logging takes place. Something similar is true of fish populations (although recent research indicates that external environmental events may be the most important and variable force affecting the fluctuations in fish stocks). The incidence of wind and sunlight is essentially independent of its use by humans. The fertility of crop land is affected by its use; as a consequence, interest in ways of maintaining fertility goes back thousands of years. More recently we have learned that underground pools of drinking water, though naturally renewed, can be badly damaged by deposits of toxic waste. Economists have worked out ways of taking account of various forms of renewability, but new questions keep popping up.

Obviously, renewable resources do not pose the same obstacle to long-term sustainability as do non-renewable resources. They are not, however, problem free. It is possible to fish a particular population so intensely that its very survival becomes doubtful. Even land can be degraded beyond recovery by the intrusion of industrial wastes. The difference is that the problem is institutional rather than intrinsic, a matter of inducing better management practices rather than merely adjusting. I will come back to this point in the next few paragraphs.

An interesting idea that combines attention to renewable and non-renewable resources is the 'backstop technology'. For example, an industry or whole economy is currently using and using up a non-renewable resource. The prospect is for rising costs, because it is efficient to use the low-cost deposits before the higher-cost ones. Suppose there is an alternative technology that produces the same final output, but is based on a renewable resource. Currently this technology is very expensive to use, more costly than the one based on a non-renewable resource; but the prospect is that the renewable ('backstop') technology will be improved as time goes on, through research and experience. An ideal management program would be to plan the use of the non-renewable resource so that it phases out just at the instant that it becomes more costly than the backstop technology. This is too good to be true, of course, but it is an indication of how one can think carefully about the transition to sustainability.

ENVIRONMENTAL AMENITY

Many environmental amenities can be thought about in the same way as the services of renewable resources. Clean air and water do not reproduce in the fashion of living plants and animals. They can and do, however, regenerate naturally by physical and chemical processes after human use. They become policy problems mainly as a result of institutional failures, in particular because of the absence of well-defined property rights.

We might normally expect the sole owners of a mineral deposit or of a fish pond to think carefully about the fact that current use of the resource affects the options for future use. Economists say that he or she 'internalizes' the future costs (or benefits) that arise from today's decisions about mineral extraction or fish harvest. To mention another example, logging companies normally replant trees as they cut standing timber. The situation is quite different in the case of the atmosphere. No one owns it. The operator of a business might rationally choose to save some costs by emitting waste into the ambient air: the cost savings are private profit, but one polluter's negative effects on air quality are dissipated over a large neighborhood, and hardly felt by anyone. The problem arises when everyone does the same. Those (cost-inflicting) effects of one person's or firm's decisions on the profit or well-being of another are called (negative) 'external' effects or just 'externalities'. They often arise from the absence of property rights. The owner of a fish pond would not overfish (except perhaps through ignorance or carelessness), but an open-access ocean fishery is in constant danger of overfishing because it is in the interest of each commercial fisherman to get what he can while he can, before other fishermen do. It would take some form of collective action, enforceable collective action, to internalize the problem. This may be local cooperation, enforced by a widely accepted social norm, or public policy, enforced by law.

CONCLUDING REMARKS

I hope that it emerges from this discussion that there is not a separate and distinct economics of natural and environmental resources. The basic economic principles that apply to these interesting and important aspects of social life are the same principles that apply to economic problems in general. But they have to be adapted to the particular circumstances that arise when we try to think carefully about interactions between nature and the human economy. In the case of exhaustible resources, the striking feature is that the use of a more or less fixed and finite amount of valuable stuff has to be spread out over a very long time, whose end cannot be foreseen. (The intrinsic difficulty of thinking about the very distant future also comes up in dealing with climate change, without the exhaustible-resource aspect.) When it comes to renewable resources, the finiteness aspect disappears, but the interaction of current use and the mechanism of self-renewal has to be understood and factored into discussions of management policy, both private and public. In environmental issues, it is usually the externalities that play the central role: the fact that unregulated use allows self-interested individuals to use environmental benefits while bearing no responsibility for the costs that their use imposes on other individuals or on the environment at large.

In thinking about policy in these contexts, the temptation is always to propose that some expert central body should decide on the appropriate pattern of use of the resources, and impose it on the individuals and firms actually engaged in resource-using activities. Sometimes this sort of direct-control policy is necessary and appropriate. I have already invoked the Parthenon and the Grand Canyon as unique and irreplaceable resources whose use has to be carefully regulated. To make a more prosaic case, there are industrial and medical wastes that are so toxic that their handling has to be controlled in detail.

Most of the time, however, the preferred policy makes use of market mechanisms. The main reason for this is that the information needed to formulate an efficient pattern of resource use is diffused around the economy and not available to any central body. An instructive example is the cap-and-trade policies in use in Europe and America to limit certain air pollutants. A central body can indeed have a view of the total amount of a given pollutant that the atmosphere can tolerate, but it cannot hope to assign a quota to each and very factory and generating station. To do that intelligently would require an impossible amount of information about local costs. The solution is to create just the right total of 'emission permits' and distribute them (by formula, or perhaps by auction) to potential emitters. A market is then created, in which permits can be bought and sold at a market price. Those producers who can cheaply reduce their emissions will be motivated to do so, and profit by selling their permits to producers who cannot. Catch quotas for fish can be dealt with similarly. Of course, many other tax and subsidy schemes can be designed to fit particular circumstances.

FURTHER READING

For anyone who would like to read further, I recommend:

Dasgupta, Partha. 1990. The environment as a commodity. In *Oxford Review of Economic Policy*, 6 (1), 51–67.

And an elementary textbook:

Hartwick, John, and Olewiler, Nancy. 1986. *The Economics of Natural Resource Use*. New York: Harper and Row.

Chapter 8
John F. Nash Jr.

BIOGRAPHY

JOHN F. NASH JR., USA

ECONOMICS, 1994

Immortalized in the biography later made into a film A Beautiful
Mind, *mathematician John Forbes Nash Jr. is undoubtedly the
most well-known exponent of game theory in economics, but he
shared the 1994 Nobel Prize in Economics with John C. Harsanyi
and Reinhard Selten 'for their pioneering analysis of equilibria
in the theory of non-cooperative games'.*

Nash highlighted the distinction between cooperative games, in which players can make binding agreements, and non-cooperative games, where such agreements are not feasible. He also developed the 'Nash equilibrium' concept for non-cooperative games, which is reached if all parties have an optimum strategy relative to each other that could not be improved unilaterally.

His work has provided insight into the forces of chance inside complex systems outside the sphere of economics. His theories are used in computing, artificial intelligence, evolutionary biology, accounting, politics, and military theory. As a mathematician, he has produced invaluable work, mostly in the field of algebraic geometry, including the Nash embedding theorem for manifolds. He also worked on differential equations and singularity theory. Papers declassified by the National Security Agency only in 2011 showed he had proposed an encryption/decryption device for military codes in the 1950s that was years in advance of its time.

Nash was born in Bluefield, West Virginia, in June 1928, and his standard education was supplemented by his parents (his father was an electrical engineer and his mother was a schoolteacher). They arranged for him to take advanced mathematics courses at a local college while still at high school.

Nash received a scholarship to the Carnegie Institute of Technology (now Carnegie Mellon University) in Pittsburgh, Pennsylvania. Initially he studied chemical engineering, but switched first to chemistry and then mathematics. He gained both his bachelor and master degrees in 1948 and left with a letter of recommendation from his tutor Richard Duffin which simply stated: 'This man is a genius'.

As a result, Nash was accepted at Harvard but Princeton University outbid them with an offer of the John S. Kennedy Fellowship.

During the late 1950s he began to show signs of paranoid schizophrenia, and spent several months in hospitals on an involuntary basis. He continued to work during his more lucid periods, but his illness persisted. By the late 1960s he says he was more or less delusional, but his behavior was moderate enough to evade the attention of doctors. He avoided conventional medicine and over time he used rational argument to rid himself of his delusions starting, he says, by rejecting political thought as 'a hopeless waste of intellectual effort'.

More recently he has enjoyed a return to form that has seen him continue his work and have a side career as a popular after-dinner speaker. With that return has come a celebratory flurry of awards and honorary degrees.

Nash taught math at the Massachusetts Institute of Technology from 1951 to 1958. He resigned when symptoms of his illness became apparent. He eventually returned to Princeton, where he has an office, and continues to conduct research.

Nash is married and has two children.

Research Studies Approaching Cooperative Games with New Methods

The general area of 'cooperative games' has been under attention as a topic for game theoretical studies since the publication of von Neumann and Morgenstern's *Theory of Games and
Economic Behavior* (1944). However, it has been an area of
difficulties as well as of some creative ideas.

In the early 1950s Nash published three papers in the journal *Econometrica* that were concerned with this area. These
specifically consider games of two persons in which cooperative optimization is the concern. First, his article 'The bargaining problem' finds an axiomatic approach leading to a
definite formula for, effectively, the canonical arbitration of
a bargaining problem in which two players (or participants)
have the possibility of gaining mutual benefits if they can
agree on a formula for cooperation. Then the article 'Two-
person cooperative games' reviews the bargaining theory in
a more general context where the two players have a variety of actions that they can take, before they are cooperating
at all, which can variously affect their welfare circumstances
(or their 'payoffs'). A fresh approach to the bargaining problem side of this total cooperative game problem shows how
a 'game of demands', for the two players, has a natural equilibrium that leads to the previously inferred formula for the
allocation of payoffs in the simpler 'bargaining problem'
topic that Nash had studied earlier. The other concept, that
of 'threats', links the competitive/non-cooperative side of the
general game of two parties with the cooperative side, which
is modulated through the 'demands' of the players. A set of
axioms is introduced that, as an alternative, leads to the same
found cooperative game solution in a fashion parallel to the

derivation of the normative bargaining solution found in 'The bargaining problem'.

The third publication in *Econometrica* was published as a work by three co-authors – Mayberry, Nash, and Shubik – titled 'A comparison of treatments of a duopoly problem'. This paper considers a concretely described situation where two producers are making the same marketable commodity. The Cournot solution for that situation can be compared with this, but the Cournot solution gives the producers less reward than what they get when they can agree upon some effectively cartel-like or OPEC-like approach to their marketing challenges. The cooperative theory gives a model of how they can profit more, and this is studied either with or without their being able to use 'side payments' in their cartel-like collaboration.

THE CHALLENGE OF GAMES WITH MORE THAN TWO PLAYERS

Since around 2000 I have been pursuing a research project that seeks to study the area of cooperative games through a process of reduction to games in the non-cooperative form where the studying of equilibrium strategies and of the consistent equilibrium behavior (of the players) is an effective approach.

This is also a general topic of studies in which a few notable researchers have been developing new ideas in more recent years. There are formulae, developed by Lloyd Shapley and by David Schmeidler, which lead to optional resolutions of the problem of 'arbitrating', by an imaginable arbitrator, of the payoff potentials of a game described by a 'characteristic function' (CF). Thus 'arbitration schemes' are available, should the players of a cooperative game (of CF type) conceivably agree to an arbitration. (This terminology 'arbitration scheme' was originally introduced by Luce and Raiffa in 1957 in their book on game theory.)

However, as soon as we consider all the ideal benefits that could derive from a good arbitration scheme, one that is regarded as acceptable by all of the parties in a situation having the form of a cooperative game, we can see that the existence of alternative schemes that differ in their suggestions for the putative evaluation of the game (or the recommended 'imputation' for an acceptable arbitration of the values of the game) leads to a conflict that brings into question all of the non-equivalent schemes.

So the theoretical question of finding a proper evaluation theory for general cooperative games appears not to be simple, *unless* we can be persuaded to accept one of the existing evaluation proposals (for such games) as the sought solution.

PRO-COOPERATIVE GAMES AS A CONCEPT

When I began, in the latter years of my life, to think again about game theory and about the challenge of cooperative games (where John Harsanyi, and Shapley and I had earlier contributed some ideas), I started out by thinking that one should look for a theory that would be applicable to any game of this general category, and in particular to any CF game (to introduce a terminology for games completely described by a characteristic function, as were the games considered in von Neumann and Morgenstern's *Theory of Games and Economic Behavior*).

But as I studied the possible situations more freshly, and as I saw how these varying circumstances of possible games related to models in which equilibria of behavior would give rise to concepts of 'solutions' for the games, I came to the realization that just like in games presented a priori as non-cooperative games, there could be alternative and non-equivalent equilibria deriving from the idea of the individual rational behavior of the players. In a nutshell, it could be like social behavior, or politics, where it seems natural that various non-equivalent arrangements of alliances of human players may be more or less equally consistent. (Effectively, this phenomenon of alternative modes of cooperation for the players in a game was noticed mathematically, when the smooth graph describing the cooperative behavior of the players in a model for cooperation of three players via 'agencies' and 'acceptances' failed to be continuable when one or two of the coalitions having only two members became too strong in comparison with the 'grand coalition' of all three of the players in the game.)

WHEN THREE-PLAYER GAMES MIGHT
BE PRO-COOPERATIVE

If we consider, for simplicity, games of three players that are defined by the specification of a characteristic function for the game, then, in this familiar category of games, we can ask which of them should intrinsically favor that the players will be induced to cooperate similarly to how they might behave if they were in a simple (generalized) bargaining problem game with three players. Suppose that, for a CF game of three players, that $v(1,2,3) = 1$ and that $v(1,2) = b3$, and $v(1,3) = b2$, and $v(2,3) = b1$. (This is the cyclical notation of $b1$, $b2$, and $b3$ that was used in my 2008 paper in the *International Game Theory Review (IGTR)*). (Also, $v(k)$, for any single player Pk alone, should be zero.) If $b1$, $b2$, and $b3$ are all much smaller than $+1$ then this is the zone where the nucleolus, or also some of the evaluation suggestions derived through the 'random proposals' models, will assign to the game the evaluation of $(1/3, 1/3, 1/3)$ while, on the other hand, the Shapley value assigns an evaluation linearly dependent on the numbers $b1$, $b2$, and $b3$.

HOW SOME GAMES MIGHT NOT BE
PRO-COOPERATIVE

A specified game may also have intrinsic characteristics that make it plausible that, even though it is a cooperative game in that the players are regarded as free to undertake all sorts of cooperative acts of collaboration (outside of the formal structure of the presentation of the game), they might *naturally* not act in a simple pattern of cooperation (and the sharing, somehow, of wealth and resources), but rather there might be various differing forms of behavior that could possibly emerge as the observable behavior of the players. This is analogous to the patterns observed in international politics and warfare, where shifting alliances and patterns of opposition have emerged regularly, for example, in European history. So the 'stable sets' or 'solutions' in the von Neumann and Morgenstern theory do indeed seem (to me) to form a parallel with what I now find to be theoretically plausible for varieties of cooperative games, that do not seem so structured as to naturally lead players to settle into a specific pattern of cooperation and the sharing of resources. The stable sets can be extremely complex in structure (and perhaps difficult to use for any practical purposes, such as for deriving a useful arbitration scheme so as to escape from avoidable conflict).

Consider the simple case of cooperative games of three persons. Let a characteristic function describe the game, with this normalized so that $v(i)=0$, $v(1,2,3)=1$, $v(1,2)=b3$, $v(1,3)=b2$, and $v(2,3)=b1$. Then, if all of b1, b2, and b3 are (comparatively) small, probably the game is naturally 'pro-cooperative'. Therefore, if this theme of general cooperation is realized, it is natural for the players to act cooperatively, more or less as if they all had to come to an unanimous agreement, so as to avoid the losses naturally deriving from failure to act well and to get mutual benefits (thus these cases can form a natural extension of the bargaining problem class of two party games).

CAN THE SPECIFIC MODE OF COOPERATION BE PREDICTED?

Game theorists are getting closer to the objective – in relation to a game that could be classified as of cooperative type – of not only being able to classify it as being naturally promoting of cooperative compromises by the players, but also being able to give to the players some good counsel about the specific variety of cooperation that might be practically achieved.

But, in principle, there can be a multitude of prescriptions for cooperation that might be created (as if) by a wide variety of various healers or therapists. For example, a 'Banzhaf value' might be prescribed to advise members of a legislative body on how their powers in coalitions should be appraised. But, in competition with this, an approach based on the Shapley value could give a different advisory perspective to the same legislators. Also, either the nucleolus, or possibly the 'modified nucleolus' might be used for a generally applicable doctrine advising on the evaluation of games.

For an arbitration scheme it may be needed only that the scheme should be accepted and followed, perhaps with an analogy to religious law. But private parties will tend to be most accepting of an opportunity for arbitration if they can feel that it provides an easier and more economical route to the sort of justice they might expect to find, on average, as the result of going through a more difficult process to ultimately reach a cooperative compromise.

EFFORTS TO REDUCE COOPERATIVE GAMES TO NON-COOPERATIVE GAMES

I, myself, in recent years, have been one of the game theorists who have sought to (somehow) reduce three-person cooperative games to non-cooperative games so that equilibrium methods could be applied to these games. The ultimate objective could be merely to estimate 'values' for the players or, conceivably, to obtain predictions as to which of the coalitions might tend to form in intermediate negotiations of the players. A group of these approaches depend on the device of 'random proposers' to achieve the descent from the level of the difficulties suggested by three-party games in general to the level of non-cooperative games of three players.

The method is very effective as it works out in practice, it seems. And, in particular, with the approach of Armando Gomes, the outcomes, as 'evaluations' for games, seem to lead either to equivalence with the Shapley value or with the nucleolus, with which of these cases being the result depending on the ratio $(v(1,2)+v(1,3)+v(2,3))/v(1,2,3)$, which depends simply on the characteristic function relating to the game.

I have also had an idea that exploits a process for relating the challenge of the cooperative game of three persons to a non-cooperative game of the type of repeated games. This repeated game is designed to be analogous to the non-cooperative repeated games which, for example, can transform a game of hopelessly conflicted players (as in a prisoner's dilemma game) into a game in which a mutually favorable equilibrium – a project supported by the National Science Foundation and assisted by the aid of three students at Princeton University who were successively involved with the NSF project. The paper published on that study is called 'The agencies method for modeling coalitions and cooperation in games' and it appeared in vol. 10, no. 4, of the 2008 issue of the *IGTR*.

PLANS FOR FURTHER STUDY ON THE COMPUTATIONAL LEVEL

The work I reported in the article in the *IGTR* journal led also to my involvement in a study of experimental games. In the experiments it was found that it was possible to preserve and utilize 'the method of acceptances' in a general sense, so that coalitions were formed always by a process in which one player or one leader of an established coalition (or alliance) would elect to 'accept' the leadership of another player or coalition leader.

In terms of the design of the experiments, the players of a game, as experimental subjects, were not told how they must or should react to the observed behavior of the other players with whom they were interacting over and over in the playing of the experimental repeated games. Of course, the design idea was that, analogous to a repeated game derived from a staged game of prisoner's dilemma form, it would be possible for the experimental player-subjects to interact among themselves, in repeated play, so that each player would tend to encourage cooperativeness by rewarding behavior (of a reactive sort) that would have comparably cooperative values.

THE RELATED STUDIES OF COOPERATIVE GAMES THROUGH EXPERIMENTS

A group of four researchers designed and carried through a program of experiments that studied the behavior of subjects who were given the player's position of being in a three-parties game, with potential rewards specified by a characteristic function defined for the coalitions possible as a result of the play in the game (which was preceded by actions of acceptance and by actions of the specification of rewards, when final coalescence would be achieved). Sometimes only a coalition of two players would result because of gambling tendencies of the players; and then each of the two players was, simply for simplicity, granted one-half of the value (according to the characteristic function) of that coalition formed by the two of them as two coalition members. I hope to move beyond this simplification in a more refined modeling for the repeated game.

The four researchers were Rosemarie Nagel, John F. Nash, Jr., Axel Ockenfels, and Reinhard Selten. The actual experiments proceeded in a 'lab' at the University of Cologne. I want to say that it is very valuable in principle that the observations derived from one set of experiments – possibly motivated by one theoretical model relating to bargaining or cooperative play and negotiations – will naturally often shed light on other variously differing theoretical models. So here our prospective study of a repeated game model, leading to calculations with, perhaps, 69 variables, was inspired by the results of experiments and their relations to a repeated game model with 42 variables (for the calculations).

THE ARRAY OF VARIABLES EXPECTED TO BE INTERRELATED IN SIMULTANEOUS EQUATIONS IN A NEW MODEL FOR THE REPEATED GAME-PLAY WITH THREE PLAYERS

I had written out, after this paragraph heading, a description about how a set of 69 equations in 69 real variables might be used in a computational model forming a refinement (and partially a correction) of the model that was the basis for my publication in the December 2008 issue of the *IGTR*. But in truth it is not quite realistic to try to describe the variables until more work has been done on developing the equilibrium equations describing how a type of equilibrium can describe cooperative resolutions (in contexts of repeated games), of the 'singularity' of game situations like those of the prisoner's dilemma variety.

In the projected work we would be dealing with a model of indefinitely repeated games having continuously variable pure strategies (for each player). The strategy parameters for each player would relate either to how he/she would act beneficially in relation to other players; or to how he/she would act in a punishing fashion in reaction to observed undesired qualities of the behavior of another player, as that player would act representing himself or herself; or as that player would act as the agent (leader) representing two players.

This is the same as we had in the model studied computationally before but now we would be providing for a more complex array of basic reactions. One agency or player could react positively or negatively to how a co-existing player or agency would behave with regard to acceptance occasions (of the second party accepting the first party by awarding agency power to the first party).

The ninth game in the series of chosen experimental games, which were researched in the laboratory at the University of Cologne, when studied mathematically (with the model that was studied in my paper in the *IGTR*), revealed a specific mathematical failure. The numbers obtained for the calculated model solution for that game had two probabilities evaluated as negative real numbers! These were the probability of Player 3 taking an action to 'accept' the coalition of P1 and P2 when that coalition was led, first by Player 1, and second, by Player 2. And this is contradictory to the basic interpretation of probabilities.

We are hoping that we can structure the options of the players for 'demands' relating to other players so that simultaneously players or agents always are making demands relating to the 'counter-acceptance' behavior of other players (that the party of the first part *could* accept as an available option). Then since this can, naturally, mathematically, call for that counter-acceptance probability to be a positive number, a side effect will be to require – in the equations to be used for the computations – that that probability will be a positive number.

Indeed, we are hoping to find here, via the route of studying some 'experimental mathematics', some enlightenment on the feasibility and value of this variety of natural modeling in terms of evolutionary cooperation.

REFERENCES

Luce, R. D. and Raiffa, H. 1957. *Games and Decisions: Introduction and Critical Survey.* New York, Wiley.

Mayberry, J. P., Nash, John F. Jr., and Shubik, M. 1953. A comparison of Treatments of a duopoly situation. *Econometrica* 21, 141–154.

Nash, John F. Jr. 1950. The bargaining problem, *Econometrica* 18, 155–162.

———. 1953. Two-person cooperative games. *Econometrica* 21, 128–140.

———. 2008. The agencies method for modeling coalitions and cooperation in games.

International Game Theory Review 10(4), 539–564.

Remark: my paper, listed above, has a few basic references to relevant works that engage in methods for approaching the study of cooperation (in games where cooperative actions of the players are presumed possible and permissible) by the use of methods of study involving modeling with the use of models derived from non-cooperative game ideas. So those included references can be recommended.

Von Neumann, John and Morgenstern, Oskar. 1944. *Theory of Games and Economic Behavior.* Princeton: Princeton University Press.

Chapter 9
Oliver E. Williamson

BIOGRAPHY
OLIVER E. WILLIAMSON, USA
ECONOMICS, 2009

Economic theory generally revolves around the activity of markets, but markets can function only if contracts can be negotiated and enforced within organizations, be it the largest corporation or the smallest household. The 2009 Nobel Prize in Economics was shared between Elinor Ostrom and Oliver E. Williamson for their separate analyses of economic governance. Williamson's studies examined why some companies grow, creating tiered management to control different but related business fields while others remain independent, despite being interdependent.

His work is inspired by 1991 Laureate Ronald Coase's insistence that the long tradition in economics of assuming transaction costs to be zero needs to be supplanted by the study of economic organizations where transaction costs are positive and vary in systematic ways to which economic reasoning can be applied.

Roughly, transaction costs are to economics what friction is to the physical sciences. Albeit convenient for starters to assume the absence of friction in both physics and economics, as theory turns to applications provision for frictions (positive transaction costs) is expressly needed. Inasmuch, moreover, as markets and hierarchies both experience frictions, the challenge is to examine these in comparative terms and ascertain which enjoys the transaction cost advantage for a particular set of transactions and why. That sounds tedious and sometimes it is. It is nonetheless noteworthy that Transaction Cost Economics is an empirical success story and has had numerous applications to public policy.

Williamson explained that there is no point in being able to resolve conflicts that never arise. If it is easy and cheap to arrange transactions – such as 'outsourcing' – there is little need for a firm. And if both parties can easily find other suitable trading partners, the firm is again superfluous.

According to Williamson, large private corporations prosper to the benefit of all parties if they observe the rules of the game (as determined by the polity) and make informed make-or-buy decisions (as determined by the attributes of transactions). Their existence will be called in question only if they fail to deliver or if they abuse their power.

Oliver Eaton Williamson was born in Superior, Wisconsin, in September 1932. He attended the local school and he was, he says, 'forever curious about how things worked (or didn't work), which led me to identify lapses or anomalies'.

He earned his bachelor's degree from the MIT Sloan School of Management in Massachusetts in 1955. After working at General Electric and for the US government in Washington DC, in 1958 he was granted a scholarship to Stanford's Business School, where he studied under Nobel Laureate Kenneth J. Arrow. He completed his PhD in economics at Carnegie Mellon University in Pittsburgh. There, he has said, he 'found [his] niche'. From a small group of research faculty and their students during the late 1950s and 1960s, four faculty would be awarded the Nobel Prize in Economics in the 1980s and 1990s and four of their students since 2000.

His dissertation, 'The Economics of Discretionary Behavior: Managerial Objectives in a Theory of the Firm', was completed in 1963. He joined the faculty of the Economics Department at the University of California, Berkeley, moving later to the University of Pennsylvania. From 1966 to 1967 he served as special economic assistant to the head of the Antitrust Division of the US Department of Justice, where he wrestled with the conventional wisdom that vertical integration and vertical market restrictions were 'anticompetitive'. He vowed to return to the subject and, back at Pennsylvania, he published a paper on it in 1971.

In 1983 Williamson accepted joint appointments to three different Schools at Yale, but returned to Berkeley in 1988. He served as Chair of the Academic Senate in 1995–96 before retiring in 2004 He is currently the Edgar F. Kaiser Professor Emeritus at Berkeley. Williamson is married and has five children.

*   *   *   *   *

Interdisciplinary Social Science:
The Transaction Cost Economics Project[1]

Although many economists decided on economics as a career choice when they were undergraduates, that was not my experience. I became an economist by discovering my interests as I progressively moved from engineering to business to economics and, within economics, finding that interdisciplinary economics (which, for me, would initially entail combining economics with organization theory and later would include aspects of contract law) was an underdeveloped but promising area of teaching and research. *As events would have it*, what became known as transaction cost economics (TCE) would become one of the foundations upon which the New Institutional Economics is based.[2]

EDUCATION

Being an engineer contributed to my TCE interests in two respects. First, much of the analytical apparatus used by

[1] The research assistance of Tarek Ghani is gratefully acknowledged.
[2] The New Institutional Economics and its predecessor – 'older-style institutional economics' – are both in agreement that institutions are important. They differ, however, in the following respect: whereas older-style institutional economics settled for critiques of orthodox economics and failed to develop a positive research agenda, the New Institutional Economics buttressed its critiques by demonstrating that institutions both matter and are susceptible to analysis. Lacking a positive research agenda, older-style institutional economics 'ran itself into the sand' – important contributions from Thorstein Veblen, John R. Commons, and W. C. Mitchell notwithstanding.

engineers carries over to economics. Second, engineers are keenly aware of and expressly make provision for *friction*. This latter point is important – in that transaction costs are a type of friction that economists, for many years, were loath to acknowledge, much less take into account (instead, the standard assumption was that transaction costs were zero).

To this are added three other salient educational events. First, two of my teachers in the Business School at Stanford recognized before I did that I had good economic intuitions and interests. One of them urged me to take courses in the Economics Department at Stanford, which I did. The other recommended that I look into the PhD program at the Graduate School of Industrial Administration (GSIA) at Carnegie Mellon University, which I also did and discovered that GSIA had an energetic and talented young faculty, many with interdisciplinary interests. Jacques Drèze, who was a visitor at GSIA, speaks for me and many others in his statement: 'Never since have I experienced such intellectual excitement' (1995, p. 123). The third event is that I was invited to serve as special economic assistant to the head of the Antitrust Division of the US Department of Justice, which was also an engaging and informative learning experience.

These last three learning experiences come together in what I have referred to as the 'Carnegie Triple': be disciplined, be interdisciplinary, and have an active mind. Being disciplined entails establishing your credentials within your core field. Being interdisciplinary entails crossing disciplinary boundaries if the phenomenon of interest is of an interdisciplinary kind. And having an active mind means being curious – by asking the question 'What is going on here?' rather than confidently pronouncing 'This is the law here!' when confronted with a puzzle.

It has been my experience that all applied microeconomists subscribe to the first of these and many to the third. The imperative to 'be interdisciplinary', however, is more controversial. Many students (including those I teach myself) boggle at organization theory.[3] This is partly because organization theory is an inherently difficult subject, but also because much of organization theory is perceived to be incompatible with economics. My advice to students when they enter the organization theory classroom and open an organization theory text is to go native: by removing their economics cap and putting on an organization theory cap. Many of what at first appear to be incompatibilities between the two take on an altogether different meaning and significance when interpreted as intertemporal regularities of complex organizations.[4] Many of these regularities are consequential and need to be factored into the study of economic organization.

This is the background that informed my early research in applied price theory and, as described below, later research on transaction cost economics.

ON-THE-JOB LEARNING

TEACHING IS LEARNING

My first teaching position was as assistant professor of economics at the University of California, Berkeley (1963–5),

---

[3] Organization theory is a vast literature that divides into three categories: rational systems, natural systems, and open systems. All three regard organization as important but only the rational systems category emphasizes the efficiency benefits of choosing the 'right structure' (which varies with the nature of activity for which organization is needed). For a discussion, see W. Richard Scott (1987, chs 2–5).
[4] Organization, like the law, 'has a life of its own' – in that it learns and matures and adapts, a striking example of which is Robert Michels's famous 'Iron Law of Oligarchy': 'Who says oligarchy, says organization' (1962 [1915], p. 365). Significant organizational regularities, be they good or bad, need to be uncovered and the mechanisms by which they operate displayed – after which the resulting benefits can be enhanced and the adverse effects mitigated in cost-effective degree.

where I taught undergraduate microeconomic theory and industrial organization, and a graduate course in applied welfare economics. Never having taken a course in industrial organization (IO) meant that I needed to do a lot of self-learning, but that too had advantages: 'You only get to write on a clean slate once.' Among other things, my interdisciplinary training induced me to ask the question 'What is going on here?' when I discovered that the IO literature prominently featured technological economies but made negligible provision for economies of organization.[5] Even worse, without a technical or physical aspect (Bain 1968, p. 381), non-standard and unfamiliar forms of contract and organization were gravely suspect and commonly presumed to be anticompetitive. I knew from my Carnegie training in organization theory and from much of my early research that organization was important and was susceptible to analysis, and that this exclusive emphasis on technology was wrong-headed.

I moved to the University of Pennsylvania in 1965 as an associate professor of economics, where I was more involved with graduate student teaching. Also, as luck would have it, I was shortly thereafter invited to serve as special economic

---

[5] Transaction cost economics is respectful of economies of technology but is mainly preoccupied with economies of organization (especially with respect to when and why to use markets or hierarchies to *manage the interface* between successive stages of production). By contrast, textbook microeconomic theory implicitly or explicitly assumed that transaction costs were nil, hence could be ignored. Although this last is approximately correct for simple market exchange, where there are large numbers of buyers and sellers on each side of the market and identity does not matter, provision for transaction costs is needed as bilateral dependency between the parties (by reason of the non-redeployablity of durable investments) sets in and adaptive conflicts across the contractual interface are in prospect.

assistant to the head of the Antitrust Division (1966–7), for which I was granted leave from Penn.

PRACTICE IS LEARNING

Moving from theory to practice is also learning. My appointment to the Antitrust Division was interesting because: (1) important issues needed to be dealt with in real time; (2) my supervisors and colleagues were exceptionally talented; (3) I would soon detect an overreliance on textbook industrial organization – with its emphasis on barriers to entry to the neglect of economies of organization. This was especially evident when I was asked to comment on an early draft of the Schwinn brief: the issue was what purposes were served by the imposition of restraints by the franchisor (Schwinn) on its franchisees. Because a technical or physical basis for such restrictions was missing, the draft brief advanced the argument that the franchise restrictions were anticompetitive. My view was more cautious. Not only was it unclear to me that the restrictions had anticompetitive effects, but a case could be made that the restrictions in question served the purpose of preserving the integrity of the franchise system – additionally or instead (Williamson 1985, pp. 183–9). Alas, the principal architects of the Schwinn brief were not persuaded and invoked what they took to be the 'then prevailing thinking of the economics profession on restricted distribution' (quoted in Williamson 1985, p. 185, n. 2). This anticompetitive interpretation succeeded in arguments before the US Supreme Court.

By reason of what I perceived to be truncated and defective economic reasoning with Schwinn and earlier cases, I decided to revisit vertical integration and vertical market restrictions when I resumed teaching at the University of Pennsylvania. The graduate students and I worked our way through the literature and, some very good papers notwithstanding, satisfied ourselves that organizational economies played no significant role. I therefore decided to examine vertical integration from a combined economics and organization theory perspective. The obvious place to begin was with Ronald Coase's famous article 'The nature of the firm' (1937).

THE CONCEPT OF TRANSACTION COSTS

Coase (1937) advanced the argument that economists should not take the allocation of economic activity as between markets and firms as given, as was then standard practice, but should *derive* which activities go where and why. That did not quickly gain assent, partly because it was not at all obvious as to which basic factors were determinative for making the correct make-or-buy decision. But there were other reasons as well. Many other developments in economics during the 1930s were viewed as more exciting and had greater appeal – to include the Keynesian revolution, the socialist controversy, monopolistic competition, the convergence upon the resource allocation paradigm, and, in the 1940s and 1950s, the progressive development of mathematical economics and econometrics. Transaction cost issues were mainly ignored over this interval.

Transaction cost issues would, however, reappear in an unanticipated way in the 1960s, when Coase (1960) and Kenneth Arrow (1969) *pushed the logic of the prevailing assumption of zero transaction costs to completion*. Pushing this logic to completion led to the disconcerting result that positive or negative side effects (for example, pollution) would be perfected everywhere – because the parties would *costlessly bargain* to an efficient result (Coase 1960). Also, firms would never have occasion to own and operate successive stages of production because the *contractual costs* of outsourcing to independent suppliers *were always zero* (Arrow 1969). Poof! Externalities and vertical integration were obliterated.

Reality testing revealed otherwise: positive and negative externalities existed and vertical integration was widespread. Provision for hitherto ignored positive transaction costs would evidently need to be made, but that lacked focus and turned out to be a morass. Because ad hoc transaction-cost reasons were advanced to explain any observed contracting practice, intrafirm and interfirm alike, such after-the-fact reasoning soon earned transaction costs a 'well deserved bad name' (Fischer 1977, p. 322).

OPERATIONALIZING TRANSACTION COST ECONOMICS

The concepts of transaction cost and transaction cost economics (TCE) are sometimes conflated but are usefully distinguished. TCE aspires to breathe operational content into the concept of transaction costs. My interdisciplinary training at Carnegie taught me that the behavioral assumptions upon which neoclassical economics relied were analytically convenient but simplistic, and that organization is important and is susceptible to analysis.

BEHAVIORAL ASSUMPTIONS

To my knowledge, Herbert Simon made the statement just once that 'Nothing is more fundamental ...'. The full quotation is this: 'Nothing is more fundamental in setting our research agenda and informing our research methods than our view of the nature of the human beings whose behavior we are studying' (1985, p. 303). To be sure, 60 years earlier Frank Knight called attention to 'human nature as we know it' (1965 [1921, p. 270]). And Percy Bridgeman advised social scientists that 'the principal problem in understanding the actions of men is to understand how they think – how their minds work' (1955, p. 450). Only recently, however, have economists begun to pay heed to such views.

Of special importance to Simon were the descriptions of cognition and self-interest. Simon's position on cognition was that the usual hyperrationality assumption in economics should be supplanted by bounded rationality: behavior that is 'intendedly rational, but only limitedly so' (Simon 1957, p. xxiv). Human actors, so described, are neither irrational nor non-rational but are attempting effectively to cope. Simon further recommended that self-interest be described as 'frailty of motive' (1985, p. 305).

TCE concurs that bounded rationality is the appropriate cognitive assumption for many purposes and takes the chief lesson of bounded rationality for the study of contract to be that *all complex contracts are unavoidably incomplete*. But TCE also takes a further step. As against the common view that boundedly rational human actors are myopic, human actors (especially specialists within firms) are assumed instead to have the capacity to look ahead, uncover possible contractual hazards, and thereafter devise contractual relief by working out the ramifications (Shultz 1995).

TCE also pushes beyond frailty of motive by making provision for opportunism. This latter does not deny that most people will do what they say and some will do more most of the time. Rather, opportunism has reference to exceptions – outliers where the stakes are great – which induce parties to defect from the spirit of cooperation to insist on the letter of an incomplete contract. Strategic considerations that had been ignored for a hundred years (Makowski and Ostroy 2001) are introduced upon making provision for opportunism.

ORGANIZATION IS IMPORTANT

Treating the firm as a production function for transforming inputs into outputs according to the laws of technology is tantamount to saying that organization is unimportant. The Carnegie tradition (March and Simon 1958; Simon 1962; Cyert and March 1963) held otherwise: organization matters and is susceptible to analysis, although the reasons vary. TCE locates much of the analytical action in the *adaptive* differences that accrue to and are associated with alternative modes of governance in relation to the different adaptive needs of transactions.

Recall that I earlier referred to transaction costs as akin to friction. In mechanical systems we look at the mechanical interface: do the gears mesh, are the parts lubricated, is there needless slippage or other loss of energy? The TCE counterpart is to examine the contractual interface between successive stages of production: do the parties to the exchange operate in an energetic and timely fashion or are there frequent misunderstandings and conflicts that lead to delays, breakdowns, and maladaptation?

As against the standard approach to economic organization, TCE is a comparative contractual approach with emphasis on the following properties: (1) the unit of analysis is the transaction (the key dimensions of which are named and explicated); (2) the main problem of organization is adaptation, of which autonomous (Hayek 1945) and coordinated (Barnard 1938) types of adaptation are distinguished; (3) all complex contracts are incomplete (by reason of bounded rationality), and outliers for which the stakes are great invite defection from the spirit of cooperation (due to opportunism); (4) governance is the means by which to *infuse order*, thereby to *mitigate conflict* and realize *mutual gains*; (5) economizing on transaction costs is the main purpose of organization, which is accomplished by (6) aligning transactions – which differ on their attributes – with governance structures, which differ in their costs and competencies, so as to realize efficient outcomes.

As a result of my experience with antitrust (as discussed earlier), the first puzzle that I addressed in these terms was that of vertical integration, which I initially regarded as a stand-alone problem (Williamson 1971). Once the logic of vertical integration was worked out, however, it soon became apparent that any problem that arises as, or can be reformulated as, a contracting problem can be examined to advantage in transaction cost economizing terms. A huge and growing array of issues has subsequently been examined from the transaction cost economizing perspective, and a large empirical transaction cost literature has taken shape.

Not only does transaction cost economics have many applications within the field of industrial organization, but also to most applied fields in economics and business and to the contiguous social sciences as well. Furthermore, it has public policy ramifications in all of these applications. It remains, moreover, a work in progress (of which full formalism is one) – in the pursuit of which the participation and contributions of young scholars continue to be important.

INTERDISCIPLINARY SOCIAL SCIENCE MORE GENERALLY

Interdisciplinary social science has been taking shape across a broad spectrum, to include law and economics, institutional economics, law, economics and organization, positive political theory, economics and psychology (to include evolutionary psychology), economics and sociology, and the list goes on.

Transaction cost economics can and does constructively relate to many of these new developments, but takes exceptions with some. The propensity for social scientists to use trust and risk interchangeably is one such example – as with Diego Gambetta's contention that 'when we say we trust someone or that someone is trustworthy, we implicitly mean that the probability that he will perform an action that is beneficial or at least not detrimental to us is high enough to consider engaging in some form of cooperation with him' (1988, p. 217). My position is that commercial risk and personal trust differ in kind. Specifically, *calculated risk* is the criterion by which commercial transactions are judged – in that whether a firm will sometimes do business with a party and will sometimes refuse depends on a hard-headed calculation of the expected net gain, the basis for which can usually be displayed. By contrast, interpreting commercial decisions to accept or refuse to do business as trust or distrust, respectively, invites ex post explanations for the sign of the expected net gain, the basis for which often fails to withstand scrutiny (Williamson 1996, pp. 256–267).

A second concern that I have is with the propensity of many social scientists, some economists included, to ascribe inefficiency to activities that fall short of a hypothetical ideal, whereas the relevant comparison is with feasible alternatives. The 'remediableness criterion' (Williamson 1996) is designed to correct against such practices. The criterion is this: an extant mode of organization or practice for which (1) no superior feasible alternative can be described and (2) implemented with expected net gains is (3) presumed to be efficient. To be sure, this last is a rebuttable presumption – in that there may be unfair obstacles to some superior feasible alternatives. Such unfairness aside, an extant mode should not be described as inefficient except as a superior feasible alternative is described for which net gains will be realized after *implementation costs* have been taken into account.

Another way of putting it is this: systematic attention should be directed to the implementation mechanisms and costs that are associated with alternative worthy projects – be they public or private. Public policy that ignores the remediableness criterion has not done its homework (Dixit 1996).

CONCLUSIONS

My recommendation to high-school students and undergraduates who are intrigued both with economics, which is a fascinating field in its own right, and interdisciplinary studies is to take electives in related fields that appeal to you. I furthermore recommend that you proceed in a two-part way. First, allow each field to 'speak on its own terms'. Then ask each to inform and be informed by the others.

TCE is still very young among fields in economics – on which account TCE is less fully developed than more established fields. It has, nevertheless, made progressive headway in theoretical, empirical, and public policy respects. Inasmuch, moreover, as the social sciences deal with phenomena of the greatest complexity, pluralism in economics has a great deal to recommend it.

Try it. You may like it. That was the experience of those of us who were attracted to economics from the outset, as well as many of us who backed into economics after trying this and trying that.

GLOSSARY OF TERMS

bounded rationality: as against hyper-rationality, human actors are assumed to be intendedly rational, but only limitedly so – an important consequence of which is that all complex contracts are incomplete, which poses new challenges for economic analysis in the context of opportunism (see below).

credible commitments: mechanisms that infuse confidence between trading parties – such as sharing and verifying information pertinent to contract implementation, creating specialized dispute settlement mechanisms that preserve continuity, and the payment of penalties to which the parties have agreed upon from the outset when all else fails.

Keynesian revolution: a fundamental reworking of macro economic theory concerning factors determining employment levels in the overall economy.

monopolistic competition: refers to firms that differ from the polar alternatives of pure competition or pure monopoly, as was then featured in textbooks of the 1930s, to include firms that produce differentiated products that have distinctive identities (brand names), yet are actively competitive.

natural systems: organizations are collectives whose participants share a common interest in the survival of the system and do this in an informal way.

open system: organizations are coalitions of shifting interest groups that negotiate goals that vary with environmental factors.

opportunism: makes provision for strategic behavior, in that firms and individuals predictably defect from the spirit of cooperation when the stakes are great unless cost-effective credible commitment mechanisms have been devised (outsourcing gives way to hierarchy as strategic hazards build up).

rational systems: organizations adapt to changing circumstances in a conscious, deliberate, purposeful way through the use of hierarchy.

socialist controversy: refers to a dispute among economists over the merits of socialism in relation to capitalism that originated in the 1930s and continued for many years thereafter. Much of the dispute was conducted in normative rather than positive terms.

vertical integration: producers of final goods and services can either produce components (such as wheels or electronics) to their own needs or acquire them from outside suppliers. The former is referred to as vertical integration, while the latter is referred to as outsourcing. Efficiency purposes are served by choosing correctly between these alternatives with reference to price, quality, delivery, etc. Anti-competitive purposes are sometimes posed.

vertical market restrictions: producers sometimes impose price, service, resale, or rivalry restrictions on their franchisees. The purpose of these restrictions is often to preserve the integrity of the good or service being sold, but can and sometimes does have anti-competitive purpose and effect.

REFERENCES

Arrow, Kenneth J. 1969. The organization of economic activity: issues pertinent to the choice of market versus nonmarket allocation. In *The Analysis and Evaluation of Public Expenditure: The PPB System*, vol. 1, US Joint Economic Committee, 91st Congress, 1st Session, 59–73. Washington, DC: US Government Printing Office.

Bain, Joe. 1968. *Industrial Organization* (2nd edn). New York: John Wiley and Sons.

Barnard, Chester. 1938. *The Functions of the Executive*. Cambridge: Harvard University Press.

Bridgeman, Percy. 1955. *Reflections of a Physicist* (2nd edn). New York: Philosophical Library.

Coase, Ronald. 1937. The nature of the firm. *Economica*, 4 (16), 386–405.

———. 1960. The problem of social cost. *Journal of Law and Economics*, 3 (1), 1–44.

Cyert, Richard M., and March, James G. 1963. *A Behavioral Theory of the Firm*. Englewood Cliffs, NJ: Prentice-Hall.

Dixit, Avinash. 1996. *The Making of Economic Policy: A Transaction Cost Politics Perspective*. Cambridge, MA: MIT Press.

Drèze, Jacques. 1995. 40 years of public economics – a personal perspective. *Journal of Economic Perspectives*, 9 (2) (Spring), 111–130.

Fischer, Stanley. 1977. Long-term contracting, sticky prices, and monetary policy: comment. *Journal of Monetary Economics*, 3, 317–324.

Gambetta, Diego. 1988. Can we trust trust? In *Trust: Making and Breaking Cooperative Relations*, ed. Diego Gambetta. Oxford: Basil Blackwell, pp. 213–237.

Hayek, Friedrich. 1945. The use of knowledge in society. *American Economic Review*, 35 (September), 519–530.

Knight, Frank H. 1965 [1921]. *Risk, Uncertainty, and Profit*. New York: Harper & Row.

Makowski, L., and Ostroy, J. (2001). Perfect competition and the creativity of the market. *Journal of Economic Literature*, 32 (2): 479–535.

March, James G., and Simon, Herbert A. 1958. *Organizations*. New York: John Wiley & Sons.

Michels, Robert. 1962 [1915]. *Political Parties*. New York: Free Press.

Scott, W. Richard. 1987. *Organizations*. Englewood Cliffs, NJ: Prentice–Hall.

Simon, Herbert A. 1957. *Models of Man*. New York: John Wiley & Sons.

———. 1962. The architecture of complexity. *Proceedings of the American Philosophical Society*, 106 (December), 467–482.

———. 1985. Human nature in politics: the dialogue of psychology with political science. *American Political Science Review*, 79: 293–304.

Shultz, George. 1995. Economics in action: ideas, institutions, policies. *American Economic Review, Papers & Proceedings*, 85 (May), 1–8.

Williamson, Oliver E. 1971. The vertical integration of production: market failure considerations. *American Economic Review*, 61 (2), 112–123.

———. 1985. *The Economic Institutions of Capitalism*. New York: Free Press.

———. 1996. *The Mechanisms of Governance*. New York: Oxford University Press.

Chapter 10
William F. Sharpe

BIOGRAPHY

WILLIAM F. SHARPE, USA

ECONOMICS, 1990

Financial markets have had a bad reputation in recent years, but they play an important role in the economy by distributing resources among various areas of production, enabling firms to invest in buildings, staff and equipment. They also reflect firms' prospects and risks, providing investors with clues for their investment decisions.

The 1990 Nobel Prize in Economic Sciences was awarded jointly to Harry M. Markowitz, Merton H. Miller and William F. Sharpe 'for their pioneering work in the theory of financial economics'. Most people are familiar with the warning 'don't put all your eggs in one basket', but it was as recent as the 1950s that Harry Markowitz distilled that sage advice into his theory of portfolio choice – a 'spread-betting' system to reduce investors' risk.

A decade later William Sharpe became the guiding light among a group of independent researchers who used Markowitz's portfolio theory as a basis for a general theory for the pricing of financial assets, known as the Capital Asset Pricing Model, or CAPM, a market analysis of price formation for financial assets. Sharpe's pioneering contribution was contained in his 1964 essay 'Capital asset prices: a theory of market equilibrium under conditions of risk'.

According to the CAPM, the composition of an investment portfolio depends on the investor's assessment of the prospects of various securities, rather than his or her attitude towards risk. This will be reflected in the choice between a combination of a risk portfolio and risk-free investment such as Treasury bills, or borrowing. Investors with no special information are likely to acquire a standard market portfolio of shares.

While spread-betting reduces the overall investors' risk, each specific share contributes to the risk of the entire portfolio. Known as the share's 'beta value', it serves as a guide to the share's potential risk and expected return. The CAPM shows that risks can be shifted to the capital market where they can be bought, sold and evaluated, making portfolio decisions more consistent.

The CAPM is considered the model for modern price theory for financial markets and is an important basis for decision-making in different areas. Along with the Markowitz portfolio model, the CAPM has also become the framework for financial economics in textbooks throughout the world.

William Forsythe Sharpe was born in Boston, Massachusetts, in June 1934. His parents were academics but, with war looming, in 1940 his father's National Guard unit was moved to Texas and then Riverside, California, where William grew up with an 'excellent' public education. In 1951 he enrolled at the University of California at Berkeley, intending to study science and medicine but after one year transferred to Los Angeles to study Business Administration. Preferring economics to accounting, however, he soon changed course again. He credits two tutors in particular with having an influence on his career – Armen Alchian, who 'taught his students to question everything', and J. Fred Weston, who first introduced Sharpe to the work of Harry Markowitz.

After earning his BA in economics in 1955 and his MA the following year, he spent a brief spell in the army before joining the RAND Corporation as an economist in 1956. There he worked with Markowitz himself, who aided him with his dissertation 'Portfolio Analysis Based on a Simplified Model of the Relationships among Securities'.

Sharpe received his PhD in 1961 and moved to Seattle to teach finance at the School of Business at the University of Washington. It was there he began refining his earlier work into the paper which formed the basis for CAPM, published by the Journal of Finance *in September 1964.*

In 1968 Sharpe went to the University of California at Irvine but shortly thereafter he accepted a position at the Stanford University Graduate School of Business. In 1973 he was named the Timken Professor of Finance at Stanford. He has served as President of the American Financial Association and received many awards.

In 1989 Sharpe retired from teaching to work as a consultant to firms including Merrill Lynch, Wells Fargo Investment Advisors, and the Union Bank of Switzerland. He is married and has two children.

* * * * *

Financing Retirement

RETIREMENT

Why should you be interested in the subject of financing retirement when you haven't even started your working career? For two reasons. First, you will almost certainly receive some retirement income from a social (government) policy designed to provide a minimum standard level of living. You should understand the issues associated with such programs as both a participant and a citizen. Second, you will probably need to save and invest a considerable part of your earnings in order to provide the overall standard of retirement living you would like. The more you know about this subject, the better.

In the grand sweep of history, retirement is a relatively recent phenomenon. The average person born in a developed country in 1900 died before age 50. In 1889, when the German Chancellor Otto von Bismarck instituted the first compulsory program providing government retirement payments, only a very few people were expected to reach the age when people were eligible to collect benefits (initially 70, lowered to 65 in 1916). But times have changed. Half of the children born in the more developed regions of the world in the early 1950s could be expected to die before age 66. But at least half of those born in those regions since the year 2000 are likely to celebrate their 77th birthday.[1] Thanks to modern medicine and better standards of living, life expectancy has increased dramatically around the globe.

---

[1] Angus Maddison, *The World Economy: A Millennial Perspective* (Paris: OECD, 2001).

ECONOMIC LIFECYCLES

Figure 10.1 shows a likely pattern for the lifetime cycle of your income and spending.[2] For each of several age categories it plots the average annual before-tax wage or salary income for a consumer unit (household) in the United States in 2010, along with the average annual expenditure. While your experience will differ, it is likely to follow a similar cycle as you go through life.

In the very earliest years of your career you may spend most of your earnings, but thereafter you will spend less than you earn in order to support your desired standard of living in later years. After you leave your regular job or career, your wage or salary earnings will decrease or stop entirely. But you will want to have some sort of income in your later years. To provide this, you will need to spend less than your before-tax earnings during your working years. The social program in your country will likely do some of this for you by deducting required contributions from your wages or salary, probably obtaining additional amounts from your employer, then making payments to you after you retire. Your employer may deduct additional amounts and provide some post-retirement benefits as well. But in all likelihood you will want to further smooth the pattern of your spending over time by saving and investing some of your remaining discretionary income. To do this you will need to move money from your working years to your retirement years. Increasingly, the burden will be on the individual to make intelligent saving and investment decisions.

INFLATION

While the prices of many goods may decrease from time to time, it is far more common for the overall cost of providing

---

[2] United States Census Bureau, Consumer Expenditure Survey, 2010, Table 3.

Figure 10.1   US consumer units, average income and expenditures, 2010

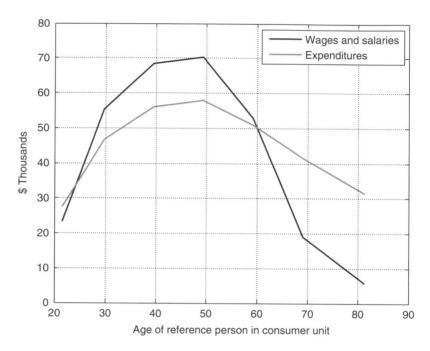

a given standard of living to increase from year to year. Such price inflation lowers the purchasing power of the currency, making the standard of living provided by a given amount of monetary income likely to fall over time.

Imagine that you were to give a bank €100 today. In return, the bank promises to give you €110 per year from now. Convention would say that you earned 10 percent on your investment. So you did, in *nominal* terms. But imagine that during the year the average prices of goods and services went up by 8 percent. By waiting a year, you increased your purchasing power by only roughly 2 percent. Your *real return* was 2 percent.

From 1980 through the latter part of 2011, the inflation rate in major advanced economies (the G7) averaged roughly

3.2 percent per year.[3] This may seem benign, but even at this relatively low rate of inflation, the purchasing power of a given amount of money would fall by one-half within roughly 22 years. To avoid losing ground, your savings must earn more than the rate of inflation.

Most of the time, securities issued by governments with good credit ratings that pay you back within a year or less have provided you with enough money to buy more goods and services than you sacrificed when you bought the securities. The *nominal rate of interest* promised by such short-term bonds or notes is likely to be greater than the subsequent rate of inflation. In such cases, even though there is inflation, the realized *real rate of return* is positive. However, in periods of high unemployment, due in part to the actions of central banks, nominal interest rates may be so low that the realized real rate of return on the highest quality short-term government debt is zero or negative.

A strategy of investing in short-term government debt may have little or no risk in terms of nominal returns, but real returns are uncertain due to unpredictable variations in inflation. To allow investors to obtain a real return with little or no risk, most governments issue *inflation-protected securities*. These are typically longer-term bonds in which the payments are adjusted to match any increases in an index of the cost of living. In real terms, such securities issued by creditworthy governments are the closest one can get to a savings vehicle that is riskless in real (purchasing power) terms.

Unfortunately, in times when nominal interest rates are low (or virtually zero), the real return on a high-quality inflation-protected security may be negative. On some days in early 2012, US treasury inflation-protected securities (TIPS) that

---

[3] International Monetary Fund, World Economic Outlook Database, 2011.

made payments over the following five years were priced to provide a real return of −1 percent per year! To obtain a positive real return one often had to purchase a security with 20 or 30 years to maturity.

In more normal times, high-quality inflation-protected securities may provide positive real returns. But even then rewards will almost certainly be small. This places a heavy burden on those who wish to save for future consumption without taking on the risk associated with non-government investments.

SOCIAL RETIREMENT PROGRAMS

Virtually all developed countries have social retirement programs. Contributions from employees and employers are mandatory and benefits are paid after a specified age for as long as the beneficiary is alive. Once payments begin, the annual amounts are generally increased by the amount of inflation, as measured by a government index of the cost of living. While these provisions may not fully reflect changes in the cost and quality of the goods and services you personally will consume, the goal is to allow you to maintain a relatively constant standard of living in retirement.

A standard measure of the generosity of a social retirement plan is its 'replacement rate' – the ratio of (1) the amount received in the year that payments begin, to (2) the recipient's wages or salary in the prior year. Figure 10.2 shows the ratios of before-tax pre-retirement incomes that were replaced by retirement benefits from the social system at retirement. Ratios are displayed for eight countries and different income levels, each expressed as a percentage of the average earnings in the country.

One striking feature of Figure 10.2 is the fact that a person relying solely on a social program for post-retirement income would typically suffer an income decrease of more than 50 percent. The other is that the replacement rates in a given country are considerably lower for those with higher incomes. This is intentional. Such programs are designed to redistribute income from higher-income people to those less fortunate.

Social programs are typically not intended to fully provide a relatively constant lifetime standard of living for everyone. Rather, the goal is to provide a 'safety net', with all but those with the lowest incomes expected to obtain additional sources of retirement income.

One might think that contributions made by employees and employers to a social retirement program would be invested, with the proceeds used to fund payments made after retirement, but this is rarely the case. For most governments, some or all of the contributions made in a year by and for those currently working is used to make payments to former workers who have retired. Any excess is typically used directly or indirectly to fund other government expenditures. By and large, such systems follow a 'pay as you go' approach.

The lack of significant true savings and investment makes social retirement programs vulnerable to serious problems of underfunding. The frequent use of questionable assumptions about the growth of the economy, unemployment, inflation, and other macroeconomic variables can lead to situations that generate pressure to reduce the generosity of such plans, adversely affecting beneficiaries. For example, in 2011, the unfunded obligation for past and current participants in the US social security system was $18.8 trillion – more than an entire year's Gross Domestic Product.[4] Worse yet, to combat some of the effects of the recession that started in 2007, the government reduced contribution rates while leaving benefits unchanged.

---

[4] Federal Old-Age and Survivors Insurance and Federal Disability Insurance Trust Funds, 2011 Annual Report. Table IV.B7.

Figure 10.2   Replacement rates, social retirement programs

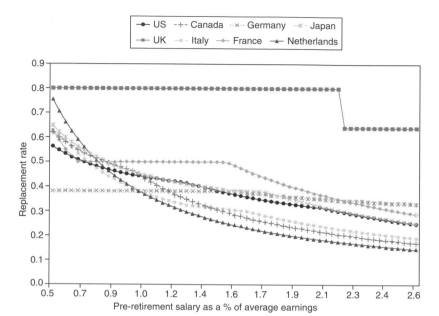

Source: from Natalia Garabato and Irene Mussio. Shaping private pensions: analyzing the link between social security and retirement adequacy. Watson Wyatt Worldwide, 2010

In the United States, and many other countries, political discussion continues about possible changes in social retirement systems. In 2010 and 2011 some countries responded to their financial crises by reducing benefits or extending the age at which participants become eligible for payments from the social retirement program.

But the problems are profound. People are living longer and life expectancies may continue to increase. Of course, no one can predict such changes with certainty. Medical advances are likely to continue to make it possible to prolong life. On the other hand, changes in habits may slow down the progress (think about fast food) and possibly diminish the quality of life. But the odds are that you will live longer than your parents, as has every generation in modern times.

Clearly, increased life expectancy adds to the costs of any given social retirement plan. But there is another factor that has greatly affected the financial status of such plans around the globe. We are having fewer children. Demographers focus on a statistic termed the *fertility rate* – roughly, the number of children per woman who lives through her reproductive life. In the early 1950s the average fertility rate was 6.07 in the less developed countries and 2.81 in the more developed ones. In the period from 2005 through 2010 the average rates had declined to 2.68 in the less developed countries and 1.66 in the more developed ones.[5] To keep a population from declining, the fertility rate must be somewhat greater than 2.0 (due mainly to infant mortality). The implication is clear. The populations of developed countries are declining. Immigration from less developed countries can help, but even those countries are growing at much slower rates than formerly.

Figure 10.3 shows the effects of actual and predicted increases in life expectancy plus decreases in fertility rates for many countries. Each bar shows the value of an actual or projected *old age support ratio*, computed by dividing the number of people from age 20 to 64 by the number of those age 65 and over. The former are thought to be of 'working age' and the latter of 'pension age', although such an interpretation may be too simple, especially in the future. In any event, the ratio is projected to decrease dramatically in every country shown. Note that all the people who will then make up the older age group are alive today, as are many of those who will be in the younger group. Without a furious increase in child bearing, a tragic decrease in life expectancy, or an unexpected massive

---

[5] United Nations Population Division, World Population Prospects, 2010.

152

Figure 10.3 Old age support ratios, 2008 and 2050: number of people of working age (20–64) per person of pension age (65+)

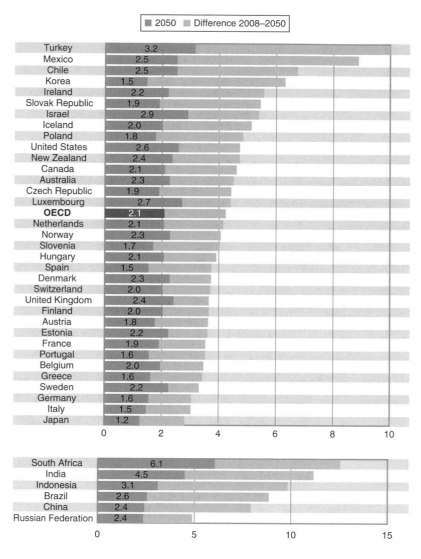

Source: Organisation for Economic Co-operation and Development, Society at a glance. Paris: OECD, 2011, Table GE5.1, Panel B

migration of younger workers from some regions to others, every one of these countries will age substantially in future years, placing increased pressure on their social retirement systems.

Many argue that people should work for more years. This could greatly reduce the pressures on social retirement programs and individual savings. Every additional year worked increases total contributions made and reduces total retirement income required. Thus far, the citizens of most countries have continued to retire at the same or even earlier ages. But in the future, economic pressures may lead many to devote at least some of their added life spans to gainful employment.

Even if you can and do continue to work later in life, you will almost certainly need to personally save substantial amounts of your earnings to finance your own retirement. And if you want to retire in your sixties, the amounts required will be large.

EMPLOYER-SPONSORED RETIREMENT PROGRAMS

To supplement or replace a social retirement system, many employers provide their employees with an independent or supplemental retirement program. In the latter half of the 20th century many such programs, like the social systems, promised payments in retirement defined in advance in nominal or real terms. In some countries, such *defined benefit* plans were, like most social programs, unfunded with benefits paid out of the employer's general revenue. But in many cases contributions were made by the employer (and possibly employees) into a fund designed to be used to make current and future benefit payments. Money in such funds was typically invested in risky securities such as stocks, corporate bonds, and higher-risk government bonds, as well as possibly some low-risk government bonds. The mismatch between the investments and the obligations led to a substantial risk that the value of the investment fund could be insufficient to pay the promised benefits, requiring either reductions in payments or added contributions by the employer.

In the last few decades many employers shifted from such defined benefit retirement plans to programs in which contributions are invested in separate funds – each designed to provide money for a particular employee's retirement. The employee is allowed to allocate his or her fund among several investment vehicles selected by the employer. At retirement, the employee can typically cash in the fund to finance his or her retirement in any way desired. Such a system is called a *defined contribution plan*, since the terms specify the amounts that will go into the fund, but not the benefits that it will provide. In all likelihood, this is how some or all of your retirement will be financed. And you will probably have to make critical decisions concerning the amount to be saved, the manner in which it is invested, and the ways in which you use the money in the fund at retirement in order to provide a satisfactory standard of living for the remainder of your life.

GOVERNMENTAL DEFINED BENEFIT PLANS

While many private sector employers have shifted to defined contribution plans, many government employees continue to be covered by defined benefit plans. A crucial issue for the citizens who must support such governmental plans is the valuation of the obligations already incurred and the extent to which the current value of the fund assets is sufficient to meet those obligations.

Most economists would argue that the best way to value such pension obligations is to estimate the cost of a portfolio of low-risk government bonds that would provide payments matching those required if every employee were to quit tomorrow. Moreover, they would say that the best way to value the assets is to estimate the amount that could be obtained if the investments were sold tomorrow. Unfortunately, due to political pressures, such pension funds often adopt procedures that put higher values on the assets and lower values on the obligations, leading to inflated estimates of the extent to which their plans are truly funded, and unreasonably low estimates of taxpayers' pension debt. In periods of recession and financial crisis, assets may be valued using averages of prices over a long period rather than current quotations. Obligations may be valued using estimates of expected returns on assets, as if such returns were guaranteed each year, instead of the more appropriate returns that could be earned at the time on low-risk investments. While the use of such optimistic assumptions has declined in the private sector, it continues with only minor reforms in many parts of the governmental sector.

In a number of countries the financial crisis that started in 2007 took a serious toll on defined benefit programs for government employees. The reality of their true funding status led to reductions in benefits, increases in the ages at which employees were eligible to receive such benefits, and other wrenching reforms. Furthermore, a few government agencies shifted some or all of their contributions to defined contribution plans, which by design have no outstanding employer unfunded liabilities and in which investment risk is borne by the employee, not the employer.

THE SHIFT TO DEFINED CONTRIBUTION PLANS

For good or ill, many private and some governmental employers have shifted from defined benefit to defined contribution retirement plans. In the latter, each employee can decide, within some limits, how much to save and whether to invest in low-risk government bonds or to put some or all of the funds in riskier securities in the hope that returns will be higher, pro-viding for a more comfortable retirement.

Why this shift? Reasons may differ from case to case, but one driving force is the one shown in Figure 10.3. Populations are aging. Under the defined benefit regime, in bad times when output falls and many people are unemployed, those receiv-ing guaranteed retirement benefits suffer no drop in income (either nominal or real, depending on the plan). When retir-ees were a relatively small percent of the population this may have been fine. But with fewer workers producing goods and services per retiree, it makes sense for the older generations to bear at least some of the aggregate risk in the economy. Defined contribution plans make this possible, but not required, for every employee. Those who wish to purchase low-risk securi-ties while working can do so, and then purchase an annuity contract from an insurance company that will provide guar-anteed payments for life. Others can invest in riskier assets and choose to invest and spend the proceeds after retirement and/or purchase an annuity. In a defined contribution regime, workers can choose whether or not to bear more risk in the hope of higher return. And the social fabric is less likely to be badly torn in rough economic times.

SAVING AND INVESTING FOR RETIREMENT

In the brave new world of retirement financing, you will very likely have to decide how much to save, how to invest the pro-ceeds, and what to do with the resulting money when you retire. If you are fortunate, your employer will provide edu-cation, counseling, projection tools and/or professional man-agement, as well as a carefully chosen range of investment vehicles such as bond funds, stock funds, insurance products, and pre-packaged multi-asset strategies. Still, your task will be daunting. Many economists have devoted their careers to trying to understand the nature of investment markets and appropriate strategies for individuals to follow when investing in those markets. Here, in brief, are a few lessons based on that research.

Capital markets are highly competitive. It is very unlikely that you will find a strategy that provides long-term returns absolutely guaranteed to be greater than those available from low-risk government securities. Most other securities are risky in both the short-term and in the long-term. You may well want to invest at least part of your funds in some of them. But understand that, at best, your eventual retirement standard of living will be uncertain and could fall anywhere in a potentially wide range of possible outcomes. If you choose a highly diversified portfolio of investments, the center of that range is likely to be higher than the standard of living you would obtain by investing in low-risk securities. But if the outcome falls in the lowest part of the range, you will very much wish that you had not taken the added risk.

The financial industry offers myriad possible investment vehicles. In evaluating them, you should keep an important economic principle in mind. In competitive markets, you will not get something for nothing. Economic theory suggests that there should be an expected reward for bearing risk. But not just any risk (otherwise we would all go to Monte Carlo) – only the risk of doing badly in bad economic times. Other sources of risk can be greatly reduced by diversifying your investments. The implication is that you should diversify widely across many risky investments so that the main risk you bear is that of a major fall in markets worldwide, due to fears of or the actual experience of widespread recessions, financial crises, and other catastrophes.

Another key principle is that you should not use your hardearned money to pay needless expenses for financial products and services. Many firms offer investment vehicles that are purported to be able to 'beat the market' in general, or in a particular sector. In return, they charge a substantial added fee every year. But both theory and empirical evidence suggest that such fees are generally wasted. The amounts may seem small (perhaps an added 1 percent of your funds each year) but their impact on the value of your savings at retirement can be very large indeed.

Fortunately, the financial industry also offers low-cost investment vehicles designed to reflect the returns in a broad market. An 'index fund' of this type simply holds proportionate shares of most or all of the securities in a market (for example, X percent of the outstanding shares of each stock and/or X percent of the outstanding bonds of each issuer). Such funds may be offered for a fee of as little as one-tenth of 1 percent of the amount invested each year, leaving you with much more money at retirement.

Here is a simple suggestion. Consider investing your retirement savings either directly or via an annuity in a combination of (1) low-risk inflation-protected securities and (2) one or more low-cost index funds representing a global portfolio of bonds and stocks. The proportions are up to you. The more willing you are to take on added risk in the pursuit of added long-run return, the greater the proportion you should invest in the risky portfolio. A boring strategy, to be sure, but one that could serve you well.

Chapter 11
Eric S. Maskin

BIOGRAPHY

ERIC S. MASKIN, USA

ECONOMICS, 2007

When seeking a solution to a problem it is possible, particularly in a non-specific field such as economics, to come up with several plausible answers. One may stand out as the most likely candidate, but it may also be worth pursuing other options – indeed, this is a central strand of John Nash's game theory, romantically illustrated in the film A Beautiful Mind.

Eric Maskin, along with Leonid Hurwicz and Roger Myerson, was awarded the 2007 Nobel Prize in Economics for their related work on mechanism design theory, a mathematical system for analyzing the best way to align incentives between parties. This not only helps when designing contracts between individuals but also when planning effective government regulation.

Maskin's contribution was the development of implementation theory for achieving particular social or economic goals by encouraging conditions under which all equilibria are optimal. Maskin came up with his theory early in his career, after his PhD advisor, Nobel Laureate Kenneth Arrow, introduced him to Leonid Hurwicz. Maskin explains: 'I got caught up in a problem inspired by the work of Leo Hurwicz: under what circumstance is it possible to design a mechanism (that is, a procedure or game) that implements a given social goal, or social choice rule? I finally realized that monotonicity (now sometimes called 'Maskin monotonicity') was the key: if a social choice rule doesn't satisfy monotonicity, then it is not implementable; and if it does satisfy this property it is implementable provided no veto power, a weak requirement, also holds. The proof of the latter finding was constructive, that is, I showed how one can explicitly design an implementing mechanism.'

Admitting his original mechanism was 'fairly cumbersome', he credits a colleague, Karl Vind, with providing a simplification. Maskin explained his theory in his paper 'Nash Equilibrium and Welfare Optimality' during his first term as an assistant professor at MIT but didn't actually publish the paper until 20 years later.

Eric Stark Maskin was born in December 1950 in New York City and grew up in neighboring New Jersey, attending school in Tenafly where he credits good teachers for his interest in mathematics. He graduated in 1968 and went on to study math at Harvard College, where he also joined an economics course, taught by Kenneth Arrow, based in part on Leonid Hurwicz's work in mechanism design. Maskin says: 'This work was a revelation to me: it had the precision, rigor, and sometimes the beauty of pure mathematics and also addressed problems of real social importance – an irresistible combination.'

He remained at Harvard to gain his PhD in 1976 in applied mathematics, but his studies incorporated a determined streak of economics, including Truman Bewley's general equilibrium course, where he first met co-laureate Roger Myerson. He went on to a postdoctoral research fellowship at Jesus College, Cambridge, where he also started his Nobel-winning theory.

Returning to the US, Maskin joined the Massachusetts Institute of Technology as an assistant professor. In 1985 he returned to Harvard as the Louis Berkman Professor of Economics, where he remained until 2000 when he moved to the Institute for Advanced Study in Princeton. Despite claiming this was in search of fewer formal duties, Maskin nevertheless also took on the position of director of the Summer School in Economic Theory at the Hebrew University in Jerusalem.

In the spring of 2012, Maskin returned again to Harvard, initially to teach Economics 1052: Game Theory and Economic Applications, and a course in social choice theory. Maskin is married and has two children.

* * * * *

How Should We Elect Our Leaders?

How should we choose the leader of our country – say, the president or prime minister? The easy answer is to hold an election. But there are many possible election methods – in other words, there are many methods for determining the winner on the basis of citizens' votes. Indeed, citizens in both the United States and France, for example, vote for their presidents, but the two countries determine the winning candidate very differently.[1] Thus we need a way to compare the various methods and identify the best ones.

Let me suggest that a good procedure for doing the comparison is first to figure out a list of *principles* that we think any good election method should adhere to. Then, we can determine which method or methods come closest to satisfying those principles.

To get started, let's look at a simple example. Imagine that there are four candidates: Aisha, Naakesh, Boris, and Wei. Assume that there is a voter named Alice (see Table 1), who happens to prefer Aisha to Naakesh, Naakesh to Boris, and Boris to Wei. There is another voter named Bob who prefers Boris to Naakesh, Naakesh to Wei, and Wei to Aisha (i.e. he has the ranking Boris, Naakesh, Wei, Aisha; see Table 2). Finally, let's suppose, that all voters are either like Alice or like Bob. In fact, imagine that 60 percent share Alice's views, and 40 percent

---

[1] The USA uses a complicated 'Electoral College' method in which there are, in effect, 50 mini-elections, one for each state. Within a state, the winning candidate (i.e. the candidate who gets the most votes) wins all that state's 'electoral votes' (equal to the number of the state's members of Congress). And the overall winner is the

Alice's ranking
Aisha
Naakesh
Boris
Wei

Table 1

Bob's ranking
Boris
Naakesh
Wei
Aisha

Table 2

60%	40%
Aisha	Boris
Naakesh	Naakesh
Boris	Wei
Wei	Aisha

Table 3

share Bob's views (see Table 3). The question to be answered is: which candidate should be elected in the circumstances of Table 3?

Let me show you first that the candidate who actually *is* elected will depend on the election method being used. In the case of *majority rule* (an election method going back hundreds of years), the candidate who is preferred by a majority of voters (i.e. by more than 50 percent of them) to each other candidate is the winner. Thus, for the example of Table 3, Aisha wins in a landslide because 60 percent of voters prefer her to anybody else.

---

candidate with a majority of electoral votes in the country as a whole. France uses a two-round system: if some candidate does not get a majority of votes in the first round, the top two vote-getters face each other in a runoff.

But the winner in this example turns out to be different under *rank-order voting*, another popular election method (it is often used by committees to elect their chairpersons). Rank-order voting works as follows: if there are four candidates for election, each voter assigns four points to his or her favorite candidate, three to the next favorite, two to the next, and one to the least favorite. The points are added up for each candidate, and the winner is the candidate with the biggest total.

I claim that, for the voting population of Table 3, rank-order voting does *not* result in electing Aisha. To see this, notice that if there are a hundred voters in all, then Aisha will get $60 \times 4 = 240$ points from the voters who rank her first. And since 40 voters place her last, she will get an additional 40×1 points from them, for a grand total of 280 points. When we go through the point computations for the other candidates, we find that Boris also gets 280 and Wei gets 140. Strikingly, Naakesh ends up with $100 \times 3 = 300$ points, even though no one places him first. Because he is a consistent second, that is good enough to elect him under rank-order voting.

So, in our example, majority rule and rank-order voting result in sharply different outcomes. Given this contrast, what can we say about which electoral method produces the better outcome?

Well, as I suggested before, we can try to answer this question by going back to basic principles. Notice first that it would be fairly outrageous if an election method produced Wei as the winner. Why? Because all voters prefer Naakesh to Wei, and so everyone would want to see him elected instead. We can summarize this logic in the form of a principle: if all voters prefer candidate A to candidate B, then B should not be elected (call this the *consensus principle*).

Now, the consensus principle by itself does not help us to distinguish between majority rule and rank-order voting. Both election methods clearly satisfy this principle: they would never lead to the election of B if all voters preferred A (indeed, I venture to say that only a very perverse election method would elect B).

So, let us turn to a second basic principle, the idea that all voters should count equally in the voting process. This is sometimes called the 'one-person, one-vote' or *equal-voter principle*. But rank-order voting and majority voting both satisfy this principle too: neither method treats one voter any differently from another. And thus we must go still further to understand the essential difference between the two methods.

A third important principle is the idea that just as all voters should be treated the same, so all *candidates* should compete on an equal footing. The rules ought not to be biased for or against any of them (it should not be the case, for example, that Aisha must get a two-thirds majority to win while everyone else needs only a majority of 51 percent). We will call this the *equal-candidates principle*. However, it is still not enough to drive a wedge between majority rule and rank-order voting; once again, both methods satisfy it.

But, now, we come to a fundamental principle according to which the two election methods *do* differ. The easiest way to introduce this principle is to imagine what would happen if Wei dropped out of the election, leaving the other three candidates in the running. I have already noted that Wei is not a very plausible candidate herself. So it would not make sense for it to matter too much if she dropped out – the outcome of the election should be the same whether she runs or not. Put another way, Wei should not have the opportunity to 'spoil' the prospects of a serious candidate by her decision to drop out.

I will call this line of reasoning the *no-spoilers principle*, the idea that a candidate with no chance of winning herself should not be able to change the outcome of an election by her decision to drop out. And majority rule certainly satisfies this principle: if Wei drops out, Aisha continues to be favored by a majority of voters to the other two candidates, Boris and Naakesh.

But let's see what happens with rank-order voting. With all four candidates in the running, we saw that Naakesh wins. With only three candidates running, the rules for rank-order voting dictate that a voter's favorite candidate will get 3 points, the second favorite 2 points, and the least favorite 1 point. Given the population of voters in Table 3 (and taking Wei out of the picture), Aisha will now have 220 points (3 × 60 plus 1 × 40). Similarly, Boris gets 180 points, but Naakesh now has only 100 × 2 = 200 points. And so the withdrawal of Wei means that *Aisha* now wins: rank-order voting *fails* to satisfy the no-spoilers principle.

As things stand so far in our comparison, majority rule appears superior to rank-order voting, in the sense that both methods satisfy the consensus, equal-voters, and equal-candidates principles, yet majority rule alone satisfies the no-spoilers principle.

But this is not the end of the story, because it turns out that there is a problem with majority rule, a problem illustrated by another hypothetical example. Let's suppose, in this new example, that 32 percent of voters prefer Aisha to Boris to Naakesh, 33 percent prefer Boris to Naakesh to Aisha, and the remaining 35 percent have the ranking Naakesh, Aisha, Boris (see Table 4). What would happen under majority rule with such population of voters? Notice that 67 percent of voters prefer Aisha to Boris (those in the first and third groups), and so Boris will not be elected; 65 percent prefer Boris to Naakesh (those in the first and second groups), and so Naakesh will not be elected. But 68 percent prefer Naakesh to Aisha (those in the second and third groups), and so Aisha will not be elected either! In this example, there is *no* candidate who wins. In other words, majority fails to satisfy *decisiveness*, the principle that an election method should always produce a clear-cut winner.

32%	33%	35%
Aisha	Boris	Naakesh
Boris	Naakesh	Aisha
Naakesh	Aisha	Boris

Table 4

Rank-order voting by contrast *is* decisive, because there will always be *some* candidate who gets the most points, and that candidate will be elected. So our comparison of majority rule and rank-order voting appears to have resulted in a dead heat: majority rule satisfies all but one principle (decisiveness); rank-order voting also satisfies all but one principle (no-spoilers).

This may prompt us to ask about other election methods. In particular, a natural question to pose is if there is some method that manages to satisfy all five principles: consensus, equal voters, equal candidates, no spoilers, and decisiveness. The answer, unfortunately, is 'no'. That answer was provided by the economist Kenneth Arrow in what is now called the Arrow Impossibility Theorem.

But there is an important sense in which Arrow's theorem conveys too negative a message. The theorem supposes that for an election method to satisfy a given principle, it has to satisfy that principle *regardless* of what voters' preference rankings turn out to be. Yet some rankings might be quite unlikely. Let me suggest, in particular, that there are cases in which the rankings of Table 4 may not all be plausible. This is because a voter's preference ranking normally does not come out of thin air. For example, sometimes it derives from his or her ideological perspective. To be more specific, let's consider the ideological spectrum ranging from left to right, and suppose that Naakesh is the left-wing candidate, Boris is the right-wing candidate, and Aisha is somewhere in between. If ideology is driving voters' views, then any voter who prefers Naakesh to Aisha is also

going to prefer Aisha to Boris. Similarly, any voter who prefers
Boris to Aisha is going to prefer Aisha to Naakesh. And, in particular, voters cannot have the ranking Boris, Naakesh, Aisha;
or at least that ranking seems pretty improbable. But notice that
this very ranking was an essential part of the story in showing
that majority rule fails to be decisive for the voter population of
Table 4. Indeed (and this is the crucial point), it is not difficult
to show that if preference rankings are ideologically driven,
then majority rule can *never* fail to be decisive.

The preceding argument leads us to conclude that, in comparing election methods, we should take account of the fact
that not all preference rankings are necessarily plausible or
probable. Instead, the class of plausible rankings will typically
be limited. Perhaps it is limited for ideological reasons, perhaps for other reasons. But one way or another it is likely to be
limited.

This brings me to some work that I have done myself with
the economist Partha Dasgupta. We were interested specifically in comparing election methods under the assumption
that individual voters' rankings are not arbitrary but limited
to certain classes.

To see how we go about this, let me first introduce the term
'reasonable election method'. Call an election method reasonable if it satisfies the five principles that we have been talking
about: consensus, equal voters, equal candidates, no spoilers,
and decisiveness. We know from the Arrow theorem that no
election method is reasonable when voters' rankings are completely unrestricted. So let's consider election methods that
are reasonable for limited classes of rankings. We will call a
method *reasonable for a class* of rankings if it satisfies our five
principles when voters' rankings are limited to that class. So,
for example, majority rule is reasonable for the class of rankings that are ideologically driven.

Our main conclusion, which takes the form of a theorem,
is that majority rule is reasonable for more classes of rankings

than any other election method. Let me make this more precise. Consider an election method besides majority rule – rank-order voting, for example – and focus on a class of voters' rankings for which this election method is reasonable (so that the method satisfies all five principles when rankings are limited to this class). Dasgupta and I then show that majority rule must be reasonable for that class too. Furthermore, we can always find some *other* class of rankings for which majority rule is reasonable but this other election method is not.

In other words, there is a clear way in which majority rule *dominates* any other possible election method from the standpoint of the principles that we have discussed. Whenever there is a setting for which some other election method is reasonable in the sense of satisfying these principles, then majority rule is reasonable for that setting too. And there will exist other settings for which majority rule is reasonable but for which the other election method is not.

What is the moral of the story? One possible lesson comes from the fact that majority rule is used by virtually every democratic legislature in the world for enacting laws. It is probably no accident that the election method that satisfies our five principles most often is also the method with the greatest popularity. But even if one ignores popularity, I think it is interesting that there is a precise way in which majority rule does a better job than any other electoral method in embodying what we want out of a voting system. So, perhaps the next time your legislature votes in favor of some absurd law, you can take consolation from the idea that although they may not have voted correctly, they at least used the correct method for voting!

For more on this topic see Partha Dasgupta and Eric Maskin, 'The fairest vote of all', in *Scientific American*, February 2004. You may also want to look at Kenneth Arrow's seminal book, *Social Choice and Individual Values* (1951).

Chapter 12
Roger B. Myerson

BIOGRAPHY

ROGER B. MYERSON, USA

ECONOMICS, 2007

*In ideal circumstances, open markets ensure an efficient alloca-
tion of resources. Unfortunately, conditions are seldom ideal. Not*

only are there infinite variables in the market itself and those interested parties, but many transactions take place within firms or other 'closed shop' arrangements.

Those involved may well have specialist knowledge they are likely to use to their advantage. So what is the best way to ensure an optimal outcome? Is government regulation called for, and if so, how is it best designed?

Mechanism design theory accounts for personal incentives and private information, allowing economists to find the most efficient trading systems, to design appropriate regulation and even improve voting procedures. The theory originated with Leonid Hurwicz and was developed by his fellow 2007 Laureates Eric Maskin and Roger Myerson.

In the 1970s, Myerson developed the 'revelation principle', a fundamental connection between the allocation to be implemented and the monetary transfers needed to induce informed agents to reveal their information truthfully, which greatly simplified the process of finding a suitable mechanism, and applied it to economic problems such as auctions and regulations.

Roger Bruce Myerson was born in Boston, Massachusetts, in March 1951 to a family that valued education and scientific learning. As a boy growing up in the nuclear age and an era dominated by science fiction, Roger dreamed of a mathematically precise utopia.

He began reading (1970 Laureate) Paul Samuelson's economics textbook in high school and gained a place at Harvard University, studying economics and applied mathematics. In 1972, as a third year student, he attended a course by Howard Raiffa on decision analysis, introducing the young Roger to the relatively new field of game theory.

Inspired, Roger scoured libraries for books and articles about game theory and was drawn to the work of John Harsanyi on cooperative theory, deciphering it until he could reduce every-thing to a simple balanced-contributions assumption. Myerson went further, attempting to extend these cooperative solution concepts to games with more than two players who have incomplete information about each other.

He received his bachelor's degree summa cum laude and masters in applied mathematics in 1973, and completed his PhD in applied mathematics in 1976 with 'A Theory of Cooperative Games'.

In 1976, Myerson was hired as an assistant professor in the (soon-to-be Kellogg) School of Management at Northwestern University, which was actively pursuing mathematical economic theory. It was here that he began his work on the revelation principle which suggests that, for any equilibrium of any communication system, a trustworthy mediator can create an equivalent communication system where honesty is a rational equilibrium for all individuals. His first article on the subject was published in Econometrica *in 1979. He continued to expand upon his theme and in the late 1980s he began applying game theory models to politics – a pursuit which ultimately led him to question American policy in post-war Iraq.*

In 2001, Myerson became Professor of Economics at the University of Chicago, where he had already served as visiting professor, and in 2007 was named the Glen A. Lloyd Distinguished Service Professor of Economics. He is married and has two children.

*   *   *   *   *

Standards for State-Building Interventions

INTRODUCTION

When we live in a successful democratic society, we are surrounded by political, legal, economic, and social institutions, each of which seems to depend on many of the others. When these institutions do not exist or are not functioning, which institutions must be established first in order to begin moving from anarchy toward prosperity? This is one of the great questions of social science. In state-building emergencies after the breakdown of a state, such theoretical questions about the foundations of the state become practical policy concerns (see *The Beginner's Guide to Nation-Building* by James Dobbins et al., 2007). One may question the very possibility of benevolent state-building interventions by foreign powers, but any hope for planning such interventions, or for holding their planners to account, requires us to have some understanding of what should come first in building a successful democratic society.

This chapter considers basic questions about the foundations of the state from the practical perspective of situations in which foreign powers have intervened militarily in a nation with an announced intention to reconstruct its political system as an independent democratic state. To focus the discussion, I will try to develop some general guidelines for occupying powers in such state-building interventions. In *The Bottom Billion* (2007), Paul Collier argues that the developed world can help poor nations by formulating various 'charters' that define standards of international policies to promote a variety of important objectives, from transparent accounting of poor countries' natural resource revenues to post-conflict reconciliation. In this chapter I want to consider a charter for custodians of democratic state-building. I will argue that, in such situations, the occupying powers should, with the broadest possible multinational support, foster a political reconstruction based on two pillars, a national assembly and elected local councils, because democratic development ultimately depends on a plentiful supply of leaders who have good reputations for using public funds responsibly in both local and national politics.

My focus on this question of standards for state building began after the American-led invasion of Iraq in 2003. I opposed that invasion, but I accepted the importance of the question of what America needed to do thereafter in order to fulfill its promise to rebuild an independent democratic Iraq. We need not have any illusions about an 'invasion to bring democracy' being good for people in an invaded country. But nations have been and will be invaded for other reasons, as when American forces entered Afghanistan after its Taliban government sponsored a terrorist attack on New York City. Thereafter, promises to help build a new democratic government in the invaded nation should be encouraged. Such promises should not be used to disguise imperialist domination, however, and we cannot hold such promises to account unless we can identify what are the appropriate policies to maximize the chances for successful democratic development.

THEORETICAL PERSPECTIVES

One argument against trying to define any general standards for democratic state-building is that every nation is different, that there is no 'cookie-cutter' or 'one-size-fits-all' plan for political development. But the real experts on any nation's political culture are its politically active citizens, and they are not neutral observers, as they have a vested interest in maximizing the power of leaders with whom they are connected. In particular, the most prominent indigenous adherents of a state-building intervention may expect to get positions of power at the center of the new regime, and so they could benefit from a constitutional structure that concentrates power in the center. Thus, a state-building mission that relies on their expert political guidance is likely to create an excessively centralized political system, which may alienate local elites in communities that are remote from the capital.

To avoid such biases, international state-building interveners (and the global public to whom they are accountable) must rely also on some general principles that are based on an understanding of the common aspects of political systems in all societies. As a social scientist, of course, I have a vested interest in the proposition that there are common general principles underlying politics and government in all societies. So I will try here to sketch at least some of these universal principles of politics. Before doing so, I should briefly indicate four strands of the literature in economic theory that have guided my understanding of these principles, but thereafter I will try to support all arguments without any technical analysis.

One strand that has influenced me greatly is Thomas Schelling's (1960) concept of focal points for determining behavior in games with multiple equilibria (see also Myerson 2010). This concept teaches us how, in a broad class of social situations, rational behavior can be influenced by publicly recognized boundaries and standards (such as a charter on state building).

A second strand is agency theory, which teaches us to appreciate the importance of incentives in organizations. But this theory raises the question of who guarantees that promised incentive rewards will be paid. Agents' incentives in an organization generally depend on higher-up supervisors reliably judging and rewarding performance. Armen Alchian and Harold Demsetz (1972) argued that the top supervisor's incentive to sustain the system of rewards for agents throughout the organization must depend on his or her ownership of organizational profits. That is, an essential role of top leadership in any organization is to guarantee the organization's systems of incentives for its agents. Agents in a non-political organization could also look to the state's courts for enforcement of contractually promised rewards, but such recourse is not available to agents in a political organization that exists to take state power itself. From this perspective, we may see political leaders as the highest ultimate guarantors of incentive systems in their society.

A third strand is the theory of reputational equilibria in repeated games. In this theory, different kinds of relationships among individuals correspond to different equilibria of repeated games, and individuals become motivated to maintain certain standards of behavior in order to preserve their good relationships with others. These models suggest how standards of behavior for recognized leaders become the fundamental laws that leaders must uphold to maintain their recognized status as leaders (for a technical model of how such effects can become the foundations of the constitutional state, see Myerson 2008).

A fourth strand is the theory of barriers to entry against new competitors, which can determine how competitive a market system actually is. This theory suggests that the actual competitiveness of a democratic political system will depend on having lower barriers to entry into political competition. This perspective suggests the vital importance of local politics, which in a healthy democratic system regularly becomes a path for new candidates to enter national political competition (see Myerson 2006 for a game-theoretical model of this effect).

From these conceptual perspectives, we may derive a general theory of political development that is focused on the essential role of leadership (Myerson 2011). People in all societies rely on recognized local and national leaders to coordinate the enforcement of laws and the provision of public services, and individuals who hold such positions of leadership are able to distribute rewards and privileges of power. All societies have ways of identifying who can be such a leader. The attributes and achievements that would qualify or disqualify someone for leadership may be different in different societies. But in any society, whenever there is competition for leadership, successful candidates will need active support from many individuals in the society. To motivate such supporters, a successful leader needs to have a reputation for reliably rewarding loyal supporters. Indeed, the key essential attribute of successful leaders in all societies may be *gratitude*, as was argued in antiquity by Xenophon, the ancient Greek philosopher who gave economics its name (see Myerson 2009). People would flock to offer their support to such a person who is viewed as a likely future leader of their community, in the hopes of enjoying the benefits of the leader's future patronage.

On the other hand, an individual who is not considered a serious contender for leadership would be unable to get support, regardless of his or her personal qualities, as no one would waste much effort on supporting a candidate who is regarded as having no chance of winning. So questions of political leadership in any society have the nature of a coordination game, in which everyone wants to get credit for supporting the leader whom everyone else will support. Such coordination games have multiple equilibria, and anything that focuses people's attention on any particular equilibrium can make it the rational outcome, as a self-fulfilling prophecy according to Schelling's (1960) focal-point effect. Thus, anything in the culture or history of a society that makes people begin to regard one qualified individual as likely to be a powerful leader can motivate rational political behavior that would indeed make this individual a powerful leader.

This theoretical perspective helps us to see how the generally recognized distribution of power tends to be self-reinforcing and self-perpetuating in a society. As a result, even a short-term foreign intervention in a nation's political system can have very long-term political consequences, unless the population generally rejects the legitimacy of the foreign intervention. The norms of any society for identifying its authoritative leaders are its core cultural asset, the key to its autonomous existence. That is why foreign political interference can be so dangerous. But the norms for identifying qualified political leaders may also become dysfunctional, as when violent attacks on opponents are accepted as normal behavior of political leaders. When a consensus about lawful national leadership cannot be found and political violence becomes chronic, then a foreign state-building intervention might seem potentially beneficial.

SOME PRACTICAL QUESTIONS OF STATE BUILDING

It might seem easy to prove the benign non-imperialist nature of an intervention simply by holding elections under a popularly ratified constitution. However, there are plausible scenarios in which democratic formalities could be a cover for the installation of a government hand-picked by foreign interveners.

When foreign forces have pacified a nation, they must be involved in establishing a transitional administration to supervise the reconstruction of the nation's political system. The interim leader of this transitional administration will need the approval of the foreign interveners; and, with their approval, this leader will be able to get his (or her) supporters strongly represented in the commissions that will draft a new constitution and supervise new elections. These supporters, expecting that their leader is likely to win the first election, could use their influence in the constitutional commission to write a draft constitution that specifies a centralized government under a strong president. Voters who are given a choice only between this draft constitution and an unspecified alternative of chaos are likely to ratify the constitution. Then the established 'interim' leader, having exclusive control of government patronage and overseeing the electoral process, will be well positioned to win subsequent presidential elections against any rivals. Indeed, many of the most prominent potential rivals may decide that they can improve their chances of political advancement by joining the established leader's coalition, rather than trying to compete against him or her. Thus, even with a formally democratic process of plebiscites and elections, the long-term political future of a nation could become dominated by a leader who owes his or her position more to foreign interveners than to domestic popular approval.

The hypothetical scenario sketched above may resemble the sequence of events in recent state-building interventions, but I am not trying to portray any existing regime as a puppet of foreign powers. My point is that foreign state-building interveners need to do more than just hold elections if they want to credibly assure the world they are building a state that is truly independent and democratic, with a political leadership that is truly determined by competition for domestic popular approval.

One important point about the establishment of the Karzai regime in Afghanistan is that, although the United States led the military intervention that drove out the Taliban, the subsequent process of political reconstruction in Afghanistan had broad international supervision from other nations and from the United Nations Secretary General. Such multinational political oversight can provide an important way of certifying that the foreign military interveners are sincerely aiming to build an independent state, not an imperialist puppet.

Now consider also the process of writing a constitution. It is not difficult to make sure that various political factions have some representation on a constitution-writing commission. But if the commission is to get anything done, one faction is likely to play a leading role in its work, and most likely this dominant faction will be allied with the leader of the transitional government. This dominant faction will then have enormous power to determine the nation's future political rules, if no alternative to political chaos can be presented to the public without their approval. But we should ask why a constitutional commission must report only one draft constitution? There is no fundamental reason why the leading authors of a democratic constitution should exercise their power without any democratic competition. An alternative procedure could allow any group that includes more than one-third of the constitutional commission to publish a draft constitution for popular ratification. Then, unless the dominant faction can win the consensus support of two-thirds of the constitutional commission, the public could be given a democratic competitive choice between two alternative draft constitutions in the vote for ratification. (The one-third threshold would guarantee that the commission could report at most two alternatives for the public to choose among. If the option of 'vote for neither' is allowed in the ratification vote, then a return to a new commission would be required only if neither draft won a majority vote.)

Even in cases where the commission ultimately reached a consensus to report only one constitution, the ability of a minority in the commission to offer the public a separate alternative could allow more balanced negotiations within the commission. So a dominant faction would generally prefer not to admit any possibility of a minority issuing a competitive constitutional proposal. But this competitive possibility could be reasonably prescribed by chartered standards for foreign state-building interveners who, as they oversee the establishment of a constitution-writing commission in an occupied nation, need to credibly demonstrate their commitment to building a truly democratic state.

The question of control over the process of drafting a new constitution is, however, only a small part of the fundamental dilemma that confronts foreign interveners who promise to build an independent state in an occupied nation. The critical core of this dilemma comes in assigning authority for the transitional government. Whoever gets control of the interim transitional government will have power to distribute patronage and build a network of supporters throughout the nation. But a national political vacuum typically exists after a state-building intervention, since the foreigners intervened either to destroy an internationally unacceptable political system or to end an anarchic breakdown of the state. In this political vacuum, the interim leader's ability to build the first national patronage network after the intervention can become a decisive advantage over all potential rivals. Thus, in handing 'interim' transitional authority to one leader, the foreign interveners may be effectively choosing the long-term leader of the nation.

One way for foreign interveners to avoid selecting an interim leader for the occupied nation is by retaining direct foreign control over the government in the transitional period, as the United States did in appointing L. Paul Bremer to head the Coalition Provisional Authority in Iraq after the invasion of 2003. Obviously this approach fails to solve the problem of reducing foreign political influence, which it merely makes overt instead of covert.

There are, however, at least two important ways for foreign interveners to pass political authority in the transitional government back to indigenous leaders without placing overall authority in the hands of any one top leader. First, substantial authority in the transitional government could be devolved to locally elected councils, to avoid giving all authority to one national leader. Second, the national administrative authority that cannot be decentralized could be assigned to a broadly representative national assembly that has the power to select the leading national ministers, and to replace them at any time, under a standard parliamentary system. In fact, the government of the USA during its revolutionary transition to independence was characterized by both of these principles of decentralization and parliamentary responsibility, under the Articles of Confederation that applied from 1776 to 1788. Recent American state-building interventions have cultivated more centralized regimes, however.

Successful democracy depends on vital interactions between local and national politics. To understand why, we need to think more carefully about the nature of democracy as a competitive system. Even with free elections, a corrupt political party could maintain a grip on power if the voters believed that other parties' candidates would not be any better. Thus, a successful democracy requires more than just elections; it requires alternative candidates who have good democratic reputations for using power responsibly to benefit the public at large, not merely to reward a small circle of supporters.

A record of using public resources responsibly in local government can qualify a local leader to become a competitive candidate for power at higher levels of government. Thus, local democracy can help to make national democracy more competitive. In effect, local democracy can reduce barriers against entry into national democratic competition.

Conversely, national political parties can also help to make local democracy more competitive by sponsoring alternative candidates in local elections. Local political bosses should know that, if they lose popular support, they could face serious challengers supported by a rival national party. From the first organizational meetings, local elections should involve representatives from two or more parties that have made a commitment to democracy. Such political parties develop naturally in a national assembly. Once a national assembly has been selected, a good rule is that any party that is endorsed by at least some minimal fraction of the national assembly should be able to participate in all elections, both in nominating candidates and in monitoring electoral processes.

We should note, however, that the formation of a majority coalition to choose a prime minister was a long and difficult process in Iraq's new parliamentary government after 2004. This difficulty can be readily understood if we recognize that, in a nation with no recent history of democratic constitutional government, there are not likely to be any political leaders with proven records of reliably maintaining constitutional power-sharing agreements with coalition partners. In an authoritarian political system, the common expectation is that any top leader will concentrate power in the hands of his or her own network of loyal supporters. So it is not surprising that efforts to build a coalition for the first transitional government may require some active encouragement by foreign interveners, as when the United States guided the selections of Hamid Karzai and Iyad Allawi to lead the first post-intervention governments in Afghanistan (2002) and Iraq (2004). But this external influence can be mitigated if the foreign interveners support the right of a majority in the national assembly to name a new national leader at any time thereafter, according to a parliamentary rule with constructive no-confidence votes.

Other important pillars of a new state include its security forces and its administrative agencies. The development of professional military and police forces is a major focus of the US Army's *Counterinsurgency Field Manual* (2007), and the development of professional staff for a finance ministry that can reliably control the expenditure of government funds has been emphasized by Ashraf Ghani and Clare Lockhart (2008). But incentives in such units and agencies ultimately depend on political leadership. If political leaders do not support the standards for evaluating and rewarding the service of professionals in public service then these standards cannot be maintained. Local political leaders have a vital role in overseeing local police. Thus, in answer to our original question of what comes first in building a successful democratic society, political development should be seen as the essential first priority that is fundamental to everything else in national reconstruction.

I have argued that the key to democratic political development is to increase the nation's supply of leaders with good reputations for using public funds to provide public services. The value of new roads and schools should not count more than this political end. When the primary goal is political reconstruction, the essential measure of success for any economic development project is how it enhances the reputations of the political leaders who spend the project's funds. So all public services and development projects should be directed by indigenous political leaders, but they should include both national and autonomous local leaders. To cultivate political leadership at all levels, foreign assistance should be distributed among national and local governments. Transparent public accounting should be required for all public spending, both by foreign donors and by the national finance ministry, to ensure that the people of this nation can learn what their leaders have spent and what this spending has achieved.

CONCLUSIONS

Questions of how to help a nation develop a strong democratic political system require us to develop a deeper understanding of political systems in general and of democracy in particular. Under any political system, power is held by leaders who organize political networks or parties by promising their supporters that loyal service will be well rewarded. In a dictatorship, national power is exercised by one leader's political network, which tolerates no rival. In democracy, different leaders with rival political networks must compete for voters' approval as the key to power. Effective democratic competition requires that voters should be able to identify two or more qualified candidates with good reputations for each elective office.

Thus, to build democracy in a transitional period of foreign intervention, it must be a time when new forms of democratic political leadership develop in the nation. The intervening powers in this transitional period should do what they can to create opportunities for local leaders to develop reputations for spending public funds responsibly, and for national leaders to develop reputations for working constructively with autonomously elected local officials and with leaders of other factions in the national assembly. These reputations will be the essential long-term basis of democracy in this nation.

From this perspective, we have suggested a number of basic principles that could be included in a charter or standard plan for democratic state-building. As a game theorist, I understand that the specific rules of the game may matter, so let me summarize these suggestions as a very specific standard template that could be applied in any such intervention. First, with the broadest possible multinational political supervision, the intervening powers could sponsor a broadly representative interim national assembly. Then, with the participation of parties that are represented in this interim assembly, local elections could be held to choose local councils in districts throughout the nation. Once these local councils are in place, the transitional national assembly could be reconstituted to include representatives of these local councils (as was done in the American Revolution under the transitional Articles of Confederation). National executive authority in the transitional period could be held by a prime minister and cabinet with parliamentary responsibility to the national assembly. In the commission that is formed to write a permanent constitution, a minority with more than one-third of the commission could be allowed to report an alternative draft constitution to be considered by the nation for ratification. Throughout this transitional period, foreign assistance could be distributed to both the national executive authority and the local councils, to broadly distribute opportunities for local and national leaders to demonstrate their abilities to spend public funds responsibly. Foreign donors should work with the national finance ministry to give the people of this nation a full transparent accounting of the assistance funds that their leaders have to spend, at all levels of government.

Our search for principles to guide democratic state-building after an international military intervention has been undertaken not to justify such interventions, but to mitigate their consequences. Foreign interveners who have militarily occupied part or all of a nation inevitably have enormous ability to harm and some ability to help the people of the occupied nation. The goal here has been to understand how they might best try to help foster the development of strong democratic foundations for the restored state.

REFERENCES

Alchian, Armen A. and Demsetz, Harold. 1972. Production, information costs, and economic organization. *American Economic Review*, 62, 777–795.

Collier, Paul. 2007. *The Bottom Billion*. Oxford: Oxford University Press.

Dobbins, James, Jones, Seth G., Crane, Keith, and DeGrasse, Beth Cole. 2007. *The Beginner's Guide to Nation-Building*. Arlington, VA: RAND.

Ghani, Ashraf and Lockhart, Clare. 2008. *Fixing Failed States*. Oxford: Oxford University Press.

Myerson, Roger. 2006. Federalism and incentives for success of democracy. *Quarterly Journal of Political Science*, 1, 3–23.

————. 2008. The autocrat's credibility problem and foundations of the constitutional state. *American Political Science Review*, 102, 125–139.

————. 2009. A field manual for the cradle of civilization: theory of leadership and lessons of Iraq. *Journal of Conflict Resolution*, 53(3), 470–482.

————. 2010. Learning from Schelling's 'strategy of conflict'. *Journal of Economic Literature*, 47(4), 1109–1125.

————. 2011. Toward a theory of leadership and state-building. *Proceedings of the National Academy of Sciences U.S.A.* 108 (supplement 4), 21297–21301.

Schelling, Thomas C. 1960. *The Strategy of Conflict*. Cambridge, MA: Harvard University Press.

US Army and Marine Corps. 2007. *Counterinsurgency Field Manual FM 3-24*. Chicago: University of Chicago Press.

Xenophon. 2001. *The Education of Cyrus*, trans. Wayne Ambler. Ithaca, NY: Cornell University Press.

APPENDIX A: LIST OF NOBEL LAUREATES

The Sveriges Riksbank Prize in Economic Sciences in Memory of Alfred Nobel has been awarded 45 times (1969–2013) to 74 Laureates:

2013 Eugene F. Fama
      Lars Peter Hansen
      Robert J. Shiller
2012 Alvin E. Roth
      Lloyd S. Shapely
2011 Thomas J. Sargent
      Christopher A. Sims
2010 Peter A. Diamond*
      Dale T. Mortensen*
      Christopher A. Pissarides*
2009 Elinor Ostrom
      Oliver E. Williamson
2008 Paul R. Krugman
2007 Leonid Hurwicz
      Eric S. Maskin*
      Roger B. Myerson*
2006 Edmund S. Phelps*
2005 Robert J. Aumann*
      Thomas C. Schelling

2004　Finn E. Kydland*
　　　Edward C. Prescott
2003　Robert F. Engle, III*
　　　Clive W.J. Granger*
2002　Daniel Kahneman
　　　Vernon L. Smith
2001　George A. Akerlof*
　　　A. Michael Spence
　　　Joseph E. Stiglitz*
2000　James J. Heckman*
　　　Daniel L. McFadden*
1999　Robert A. Mundell*
1998　Amartya Sen
1997　Robert C. Merton*
　　　Myron S. Scholes*
1996　James A. Mirrlees*
　　　William Vickrey
1995　Robert E. Lucas Jr.
1994　John C. Harsanyi
　　　John F. Nash Jr.*
　　　Reinhard Selten*
1993　Robert W. Fogel*
　　　Douglass C. North*
1992　Gary S. Becker
1991　Ronald H. Coase
1990　Harry M. Markowitz
　　　Merton H. Miller
　　　William F. Sharpe*
1989　Trygve Haavelmo
1988　Maurice Allais
1987　Robert M. Solow*
1986　James M. Buchanan Jr.*
1985　Franco Modigliani
1984　Richard Stone
1983　Gerard Debreu
1982　George J. Stigler
1981　James Tobin
1980　Lawrence R. Klein

1979 Theodor W. Schultz
      Sir Arthur Lewis
1978 Herbert A. Simon*
1977 Bertil Ohlin*
      James E. Meade*
1976 Milton Friedman
1975 Leonard V. Kantorovich*
      Tjalling C. Koopmans*
1974 Gunnar Myrdal*
      Friedrich August von Hayek*
1973 Wassily Leontief
1972 John R. Hicks
      Kenneth J. Arrow
1971 Simon Kuznets
1970 Paul A. Samuelson*
1969 Ragnar Frisch*
      Jan Tinbergen

*Laureate who attended Lindau Meeting(s)

APPENDIX B:
THE LINDAU MEETINGS

EDUCATE – INSPIRE – CONNECT:
NOBEL LAUREATES AS ROLE MODELS

The Lindau Nobel Laureate Meetings generate and promote enthusiasm for science and research and the scientists behind them. Since their formation in 1951, these Meetings have developed into a unique forum and venue for dialog and scientific exchange. For 60 years they have been recognized worldwide for their high scientific standards, while they foster the transfer of knowledge between Nobel Laureates and young researchers through international and intercultural interactions.

Laureates in Chemistry, Physics, Physiology or Medicine, and lately the Winners of the Sveriges Riksbank Prize in Economic Sciences in Memory of Alfred Nobel (commonly referred to as the Nobel Prize in Economics), meet with highly talented young scientists from all over the world at Lake Constance in southern Germany. Every summer they make Lindau and the Isle of Mainau the smartest islands in the world.

At the initiative of Wolfgang Schürer, Vice President of the Council and Chairman of the Foundation Lindau Nobelprizewinners Meetings at Lake Constance, in 2004 the Meetings added the Economic Sciences. Prior to that, several Nobel Economists participated in Meetings of the other disciplines. Ragnar Frisch, who shared the first Prize in Economics with Jan Tinbergen in 1969, began the tradition just two years later in 1971, followed by Gunnar Myrdal in

1976. Friedrich August von Hayek, who attended six meetings in all, James E. Meade, and Bertil Ohlin came in 1978; Leonid V. Kantorovich in 1979; Meade returned in 1982, joining Tjalling C. Koopmans and Paul A. Samuelson that year. Gérard Debreu and Herbert A. Simon were guests in 1986, and James M. Buchanan Jr. came in 1989.

Nobel Laureates and young scientists especially appreciate the large number of personal encounters which make for the unprecedented atmosphere of the Meetings. The intense exchange of ideas between different generations of scientists makes a significant contribution to worldwide discourse, paving the way for interdisciplinary research and scientific progress. The inspiration provided by Nobel Laureates – people the young researchers usually know only from their textbooks – is often described by former participants as a once-in-a-lifetime experience. The Lindau Meetings are about people, not papers, and it is this unique format, which serves as the birthplace of global networks of young scholars and doctoral students, that will continue to make an impact far into the future.

Count Lennart Bernadotte's vision of a peaceful exchange of ideas amongst international scientists came immediately after World War II, and was unusual not only for the 1950s. Sixty years later, it is commonly agreed that his dedication contributed to much more than international understanding. Year after year the Meetings prove that Count Bernadotte, along with two Lindau physicians, co-founded a 'factory of ideas' for the future, one that marks Germany, and Europe, as important centers of science. The Nobel Laureates Meetings have opened paths that were previously impassable and opened doors that had appeared to be locked forever.

For 38 years Count Lennart was active as the President of the Council for the Lindau Nobel Laureate Meetings. His vision of a forum for the scientific elite of today and tomorrow, one that crosses cultures, nationalities, and religions, is now the obligation and incentive for future work. His charisma made an impact on the Meetings and made it possible to establish contact with many of the Nobel Laureates. His roots are in the Royal Family of Sweden – his grandfather, who later became King Gustaf V of Sweden, bestowed the first Nobel Prizes – and the contacts he established at the Swedish institutions that award the Nobel Prizes still serve as the foundation for the Meetings.

Count Lennart was always ahead of his time. His method for promoting enthusiasm, perseverance, and passion for science and research amongst young people is just as noteworthy as his role as a pioneer in sustainability. In light of current issues in economics and society, his *Grüne Charta von der Mainau* ('Green Charter of Mainau') is just as timely now as it was when it originated in 1961: 15 years before the first state laws on environmental protection, 25 years before the creation of the German Federal Ministry for the Environment, Nature Conservation and Nuclear Safety, seven years before the formation of the Environmental Protection Agency in the US, and 11 years before the first report by the Club of Rome, the *Charta* was already calling for sustainability in the use of resources.

In honor of Count Lennart Bernadotte, the Foundation Lindau Nobelprizewinners Meetings at Lake Constance was established in 2000. Its patrons are committed to the idea of the Meetings as promoting science and intercultural dialog, and they ensure that ongoing endeavor through their donations to the endowment. Presently the 264 Nobel Laureates who are members of the Founders Assembly help to secure the future of this one-of-a-kind forum.

The Lindau principle is based on the methodology of the Nobel Laureates and relies on their personal commitment, for which we are eternally grateful. This allows advances and accelerates learning and education through a multi-generational dialog as the guiding spirit of the Meetings. It is often seen as being the leitmotiv, the theme, of the Lindau Meetings. Indeed, this is and always will be its intellectual basis, corresponding with the intention of Alfred Nobel, the prize in his name, the Laureates, and last but not least Count Lennart Bernadotte, his congenial advocate.

Nikolaus Turner
Member of the Board, Council for the
Lindau Nobel Laureate Meetings
Managing Director and Member of the Board, Foundation Lindau
Nobelprizewinners Meetings at Lake Constance

For more information and the Lindau Mediatheque: www.lindau-nobel.org.

Printed and bound in the United States of America